Building Cathedrals Not Walls

Essays for Parents and Teachers

All essays in this book were previously published as Kids Talk columns.

This book available from www.createspace.com/3399294 and www.BuildingCathedrals.net.

ISBN   1449509592
EAN-13   978-144950-959-0

For more information visit:

www.MarenSchmidt.com and
www.KidsTalkNews.com

To the children of the world

TABLE OF CONTENTS

Building Cathedrals Not Walls

Building Cathedrals Not Walls

.

INTRODUCTION

My husband loves cathedrals. Before we visited Italy a few years ago, Mark studied the construction of the cathedral in Florence, the Basilica di Santa Maria del Fiore, better known as Il Duomo for its distinctive red dome. For weeks, every morning over coffee I received an update on Mark's readings. The 140 year long project's challenges captivated me.

Construction of the cathedral was estimated to be 170 years at the time of groundbreaking. Building on the cathedral in Florence began in 1296 and was completed in 1436. Arnolfo di Cambio designed the cathedral with a dome, but left no plans on how to engineer the structure. The cathedral's dome claims fame for being only slightly smaller than the dome in the Pantheon. Il Duomo's roof stood opened for at least 40 years, because no one knew how to build the dome.

In 1419 the Arte della Lana held a competition to design a dome and cupola. Florence at this time was home to a legendary line-up of artists: the better know Michelangelo, Donatello, Raphael, and Da Vinci. Lorenzo Ghiberti, famous for his design of the cathedral's baptistery doors, and Filippo Brunelleschi vied for the honor to build the dome. Brunelleschi barely won the contest and unhappy political supporters of Ghiberti began to protest the award and Brunelleschi's design.

To build scaffolding for the dome would have required every tree in Europe at the time. Brunelleschi's design required no scaffolding and used a double layer of brick. The construction required over four million bricks and weighed over 37,000 tons.

Ghiberti worked to create uncertainty in the minds of the Arte de Lana of the engineering quality of Brunelleschi's design. Ghiberti wanted to be in charge of the dome, since it was a lucrative and prestigious assignment. Ghiberti's undermining efforts gained him the title of *co-capomaestro*, much to Brunelleschi's dismay.

Ghiberti and Brunelleschi battled over control of the dome construction. Brunelleschi won by feigning illness for a period of time and construction came to a halt. Ghiberti had no idea of how to continue. At that point Brunelleschi gained total engineering authority of the project.

Brunelleschi guarded his secrets and let the masons know week by week what shape of brick and stone to make by carving a potato in the required form.

Construction on the dome lasted 16 years, from 1420 to 1436. Il Duomo is still the largest masonry dome in the world rising 375 feet to the top of the cupola.

During this time in Europe scores of cathedrals were envisioned, funded and built taking generations to complete, enduring plagues, wars, lost funding and more.

How did people toil on a project that wouldn't be finished in their lifetime, much less their grandchildren's?

In today's world who embarks on a project that requires 140 years of construction?

Who begins an endeavor while lacking the engineering know-how to finish it?

An architect visited a construction site on his vacation. As he walked around he asked the brick masons what they were building.

"Mister," the first worker said as he slopped mud onto a brick, "can't you see I'm building a wall?"

Every worker he chatted with, no matter if the chore was laying brick, shoveling or mixing cement, told the architect they were laying brick or stacking a wall.

One worker offered a different version of his labors. As he stood upright and smiled, the man said, "Look. I'm building a cathedral."

If asked what we were doing during our day-to-day toils and challenges of parenting and teaching, we might be apt to answer, "Can't you see I'm busy with the kids?"

If we shift our perception and develop the art of the long view we should discover that we are part of a group who is building humanity. We are part of a group who strives to build a better world, task by task, day by day, year in year out, generation by generation.

When we have a plan and a vision, we understand that, indeed, we are building cathedrals, not walls. The mundane becomes the magnificent.

And that makes all the difference.

The essays in this book, I hope, will inspire you to see that we are working on something bigger than ourselves. Much bigger.

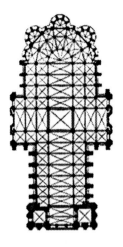

FOUNDATIONS
Love, Family and Work

---

fter a cathedral's plans were finalized the foundation comprised a community's first efforts. Cathedral foundations reached a depth of over 25 feet. Thick walls supported the building to prevent uneven settling. A foundation must be perfectly horizontal and vertical in order to build a safe and sound structure atop it.

While excavating and building footings, supplies were collected for the next stages of construction. In preparation for scaffolding needed for columns and walls, tall trees up to 60 feet in length were ordered from Scandinavia and shipped. Barges of stone floated down rivers from local quarries.

The foundations we build for our families should be deep, strong and level as well. We can build our foundations with three gifts of human beings—our ability to love, our ability to use our hands and our minds to create, and our ability to choose.

Building a solid foundation for life requires looking deep within to understand yourself and your relationships with others, creating a base much like the foundation of a cathedral that invisibly supports structure and beauty.

As we build our foundations we also need to prepare for the next phases of construction. In parenting and teaching, we must anticipate the next stage in the process of child development.

Teaching Children To Love

The purpose of the adult of the species, any species, is to ensure the success of the next generation. From bees to bears, from hyenas to humans, every adult's job is to provide for the young. Someone did it for us. Now it is our turn to give back, ideally giving more than we were given. We assure the success of future generations by teaching our children to love.

We may think our jobs and careers are solely about us and that children have nothing to do with our work. If careers are based only on our individual desires or needs, at some point we will feel that something is lacking. We see ourselves as teachers, lawyers, warehouse workers, doctors, sales managers, company associates, etc., but our real job is to assure the success of the next generation. Wherever we are, whoever we are, our job is to help others view life through eyes of love.

When we lose that connection to love, that is the moment that things start to go downhill, sometimes quickly, and other times so slowly that we don't realize anything has changed until it is too late to avoid the consequences of broken relationships, feelings of isolation, anger and hateful behavior. It is in our families that we learn to love and to express that love. Our families are also where we can learn to be fearful of the world, and learn to express fear in its many damaging ways.

Dr. Phil McGraw in his book, *Family First*, writes about helping families out of extreme conflict and unloving behavior. Dr. Phil tells these families, "You're not bad people. You've just lost your way." How quickly we lose our way when we choose not to use the energy of love.

We show our love through our actions, through our work and through our words. As Shakespeare said it in the play *Two Gentlemen from Verona*, "They do not know love that do not show their love." To teach our children to love, we must show our love. We must learn how to express our love in all its billions of variations. To have love, teach love.

Creating a loving response to the many unloving actions we encounter is a challenge. Paul in his letter to the Corinthians wrote:

> *Love is patient, love is kind. It does not envy, it does not boast, it is not proud. It is not rude, it is not self-seeking, it is not easily angered, it keeps no record of wrongs. Love does not delight in evil but rejoices with the truth. It always protects, always trusts, always hopes, always perseveres. Love never fails. — 1 Corinthians 13: 4-8*

Love never fails. For that reason, it is our most important skill to teach, perhaps the only thing we should teach.

In Service to the Child

When you help a child climb the tree, everyone enjoys the fruit. — *Nankani Proverb*

What do we expect when we patronize a restaurant? Tasty food, cheerful wait staff, good cost/price performance, timely delivery, and of course, not to go away hungry.

Our decision making process is based on factors of price, timeliness, quality of relationships, and product delivered. Our expectations at a fast food joint differ from those for a five star restaurant, but are based on similar criteria. We don't expect cherries jubilee at a taco place. If our food was wrapped in paper at Chez Louie, we might be irate. Also, we'd never ask to purchase shoes at a restaurant. We select a business to meet specific needs or desires.

When a business tries to be everything to everybody, or everything to a few people, it is apt to fail. A solitary business would struggle to meet every need and desire of every customer. Responding to over demanding customers can cause a business to lose focus, neglect clients, and ultimately fail.

The business of being parents, teachers and caretakers is much like that of any business. Our business is to serve the child or, in Dr. Montessori's words, to help the child "become a complete human being, able to exercise in freedom a self-disciplined will and judgment, unperverted by prejudice and undistorted by fear."

Things can start to go wrong in our business as parents and caregivers when, in a misconstrued sense of service, we try to meet every need and whim of a child. Instead of assisting a child's developmental needs, we inadvertently train them to be over demanding and unrealistic not-yet human beings.

Children's basic needs are to become a person engaged in their time and place, and to construct themselves as human beings who will be of service to others. Becoming a person of your time and place has as many variations as people on this planet.

As parents, teachers, and caretakers, we offer a service to our children to meet their needs in order for them to become fully functioning adults. It's a role we fill, much like the service a restaurant offers. Adults work to meet the child's fundamental needs of food, clothing, shelter, loving relationships, along with human development and learning needs, using available resources.

A successful restaurant doesn't have to meet the impractical whims of every customer. A winning business offers a good product, cheerfully, in a timely manner, at a price the customer can afford, with a desire for repeat business, and a long-term relationship.

To serve our children, we need to act like a successful business. We cheerfully attend to a child's genuine needs with the resources we have available in our culture, based on our personal values.

We will serve our children best by being the adult we want our children to become.

To Be a Help to Life

"No man is free who is not master of himself."—*Epictetus*

A flower begins with a seed sprouting from the earth with the seed leaves coming out of the ground first. The plant grows a stalk, and sends out more leaves. On the stalk or branches of the plant, small buds form and are protected by the calyx of the flower. One day when the bud is large enough, the days are warm enough, and there is the right amount of sunlight and rain, the calyx begins to open, and the flower appears.

The petals of the flower begin to unfold from the calyx. The pistil and the stamen become visible. Bees and birds visit the flower and spread the sticky yellow pollen from the stamen from flower to flower, fertilizing the plants. After fertilization, at the base of the pistil, the ovary begins to swell to produce the fruit, in which seeds for new plants are embedded.

A plant grows, a flower blooms, and fruit ripens, all on an observable and predictable sequence for each species of plant. Weather, water, time and location are some of the factors that influence the growth and maturity rate of a plant.

Humans are more complex than plants, but each human personality unfolds in accordance to a pattern of growth.

"To be a help to life." That is the Montessori teachers' credo.

To be a help to a plant, we plant it in fertile soil in an appropriate climate. For example, without a special environment orange trees won't grow in Arkansas. To be a help to a plant, we assure that the seedlings are watered, weeded, and protected from being trampled. As young plants grow, we protect them from deer and rabbits. We stake the tomatoes. As the plants mature, we check the plants for signs of disease. We prune if a shoot makes a plant unstable, or nip the buds if a plant overproduces.

As we care for plants, we don't pull up a plant and look at its roots to see if it's growing. We watch and observe. We don't have to run tests on a plant to see if it's growing normally. We watch and observe.

As the plant matures, we harvest and we enjoy the fruit of the plant, and the fruit of our labors.

To be a help to life.

Plant, water, weed, protect, strengthen, harvest. Obvious work for helping plants. A plant's success is ensured in a garden with a knowledgeable gardener.

Children need a place where they are watched, nourished, protected, and strengthened until adulthood, until they are masters of themselves.

Be a help to life. Watch. Nourish. Protect. Strengthen. Then enjoy the harvest.

Put the Big Stuff In First

A Ukrainian folktale called *The Mitten* relates the story of a lost mitten and a bear. The children in my class enjoyed this story, and even turned it into a play. There are various versions of this story, and one goes something like this:

One day a bear takes a walk in the woods when it starts to snow. The bear can't get back to his cave before darkness falls. Fortunately the bear finds a mitten and crawls into the mitten to snuggle for the night.

In a few minutes the bear is disturbed by a fox asking to join him. The bear reluctantly lets the fox inside the mitten. Soon after, a goat asks to enter. Next comes a porcupine. A rabbit. A turtle. A mouse. All the animals manage to squeeze into the mitten and are drifting off to sleep when the voice of an ant enters the mitten. "May I please come in from the cold?"

The animals in the cramped mitten look at the shivering ant and say, "Come in."

The ant crawls in. The mitten explodes, torn to pieces.

Stephen Covey on his *The Eighth Habit* DVD has a chapter called *Big Rocks*. During a workshop, Covey asks a participant to fit several rocks into a transparent tub already three-quarters filled with green pebbles. The big rocks represent the important activities in our lives—family, friends, work, vacations, education, and more. After several minutes of diligent effort to get the rocks into the tub, Covey suggests looking at the problem in a different way and offers the use of a second tub. When the participant places the big rocks in the tub first and pours the pebbles in last, everything fits.

A mitten. A tub. A bear. Some rocks. If we put the big stuff, the activities that enrich our life the most, in first, somehow it will all fit, and we'll find space for little pleasantries also. When we do it right, it's not huge issues that cause our lives to go all to pieces; it's little ants that ruin our picnic, or pretty pebbles that fill up the bucket leaving no room for vital tasks.

First, put in the big stuff. Determine what are the most important activities and tasks in your life and base your decisions on these priorities. When we put the big rocks first, we find it easy to say "yes" to the important and "no" to the nonessential tasks that interrupt us.

When we put the big stuff in first, we have opportunities to use our power of choice, clear principles, and our innate intelligence to create our lives.

When we use our imaginations, even a bear can fit inside a lost mitten, and our lives in a bit of eternity.

Family Meetings

"You want us to have family meetings with our four and five-year olds?" Our parenting group leaders were explaining how to plan a family meeting. My husband and I were taking an "Active Parenting" course to help us deal with, among other things, our two daughters' sibling rivalry. We were open to new ideas and techniques. Could a weekly meeting with children under the age of six be productive? This was an interesting idea. We listened.

Our first step was to establish a predictable time each week to have the meetings. We settled on Saturday mornings, when everyone would be fresh. The first meeting of course would be short. At family meetings there are two alternating leadership roles, chairperson and secretary. The chairperson makes sure the meeting runs smoothly and that everyone is heard. The secretary takes the minutes and reads them at the next meeting. My husband and I figured it would be years before our daughters would be ready to step into a leadership role.

The meeting agenda consists of a compliment time, reading of the minutes, old business, finances, new business, and ends with a treat. The treat can be a snack, an outing or a game.

We went home and told the girls about the family meeting idea. On Saturday, we started with compliment time with each family member giving everyone a thank you or an acknowledgement of some accomplishment or strength. The girls found it difficult to give each other compliments, so I made a mental note to help them practice before the next meeting.

We didn't have any minutes to read or old business to discuss at the first meeting. For finances we decided to discuss how we were saving for a summer trip. How much can you discuss with a four and five-year-old?

On our first agenda, we discussed bedtime routine, how to treat guests in the house, and how to include or not include your sister if a friend came over. This took ten minutes. Then we were off to the Farmer's Market, which became our routine for a couple of years.

By the third meeting, our almost six-year-old wanted to have a turn as chairperson and run the meeting. Much to my surprise, she did an admirable job. We kept our weekly agenda on our refrigerator and kept minutes in a spiral notebook. Minutes of the meetings can be very simple, for example:

Family Meeting, January 6, 1995
Chair: Dana   Secretary: Maren
Decisions made:

1. Plan family vacation.

2. Save money for ski trip.

3. Remember to ask permission to use other people's things.

In the beginning our meetings felt a little stiff and formal. In a few weeks they became more natural and relaxed. Here are some recommended ground rules from Active Parenting for your family meetings:

1. Every person has an equal voice.

Let everyone's opinions be heard.

2. Everyone may share what he or she thinks and feels about each issue.

Ask quiet children for their opinions and avoid expressing disapproval if children share unpleasant feelings.

3. Decisions are made by consensus.

Votes are not taken and majority doesn't rule. Matters are discussed until all are in agreement.

4. All decisions are adhered to until the next meeting.

Any complaints about a decision should receive the comment, "Put in on the agenda for the next meeting."

5. Some decision are reserved for parents.

Not everything is up for discussion and a decision. Parents have decisions to make that are theirs alone, for example a job change or move. Family meetings can help the family express thoughts, concerns and feelings about changes made by parents' decisions.

Over the years our family meetings grew less frequent and formal as we learned, as a family, how to handle our problems effectively. For more information about Active Parenting and family meetings, go to www.activeparenting.com.

Together

In my chiropractor's examining room, there is a poster of two hands reaching for a handshake with the title "Together." The poster says:

Our Job
See you as an individual
Respect your privacy and your time
Provide a comfortable office
Explain procedures
Monitor and report progress
Show you ways to get and stay well
Offer state of the art chiropractic
Refer to specialists if needed
Charge a fair fee for our services
Honor individual health goals

Your Job
Want better health
Get involved
Keep appointments
Follow advice
Ask questions
Seek answers
Expect results

Stay optimistic
Pay your bill
Tell others

For me this poster clearly communicates the roles of doctor and patient. Upon further reflection, I see that this message is valid for any professional relationship or organization. An organization, as Stephen Covey defines it, is any group of two or more people working for a common goal.

Excited about how this poster states clear roles and expectations, I revised it to reflect the relationships between school and home, or teacher and parents.

A School's Job
See you and your child as individuals
Respect your privacy and your time
Provide comfortable facilities
Explain school procedures
Monitor and report your child's progress
Show you ways to aid your child's development
Offer state of the art education
Refer to specialists if needed
Charge a fair fee for our services
Honor individual educational needs

A Family's Job
Want a better school community for all
Get involved
Be on time
Follow advice
Ask questions
Seek answers
Expect results
Stay optimistic
Pay your tuition and/or taxes
Tell others

Having played many roles in education—student, teacher, parent, school administrator, principal, school owner, tuition check writer and taxpayer—I realize that when I missed one of the jobs on this list, problems followed. When someone didn't do their part within the organization, trust and satisfaction in the relationship was damaged or destroyed.

In the roles we play in our educational organizations, as either service providers or consumers, let's encourage the development of clear and concise expectations for the tasks that need to be addressed to assure our group's success.

Our Job. Your Job. It's easy to look at these lists and for everyone to know if expectations are being met. When there are rough spots in a relationship, (remember, if we're human there will be problems) each party can look at the lists to help define the problem, discern contributing factors to the situation, and create possible solutions.

Roles and expectations clearly stated from the beginning can help us make our organizations successful for all our students, our families, our school staff and our communities.

A successful doctor needs cooperative patients. Patients need an understanding doctor. Successful schools need collaborative families. Families need effective schools. Together, we can do it.

Sensitive Periods For Learning From Birth to Six

Before the age of six, human beings are in a unique period of learning and development. At this time in our lives, certain information is absorbed by our personalities without conscious effort. Young children learn to walk, talk and do hundreds of things without formal instruction or being aware of learning. Dr. Maria Montessori described these stages as sensitive periods of development.

Sensitive periods are characterized by five observable behaviors. Children seem to be drawn to certain work and we see the following:

1. A well-defined activity with a beginning, middle and end,

2. The activity is irresistible for the child once he or she starts it,

3. The same activity is returned to again and again,

4. A passionate interest develops,

5. A restful and tranquil state comes at the finish of the activity.

Once the sensitive period is over, children are not drawn to certain activities as before. Three-year olds love to wash their hands because they are in a sensitive period, whereas ten-year-olds are not.

There are five major sensitive periods of development from birth to age six: Language, Order, Refinement of the Senses, Movement and Social Relations. Here we'll talk about social relations and the following sections will focus on the other four sensitive periods.

Between ages two-and-a-half to four-and-a-half years children are learning social skills and manners that will be the foundation for their social interactions. Between the ages of 12 to 15, there is another developmental period when young teens are open to developing and polishing social skills. This is one reason that dance lessons and cotillion are offered at this age.

Between ages three to six, children are learning social cues, such as, when to say please and thank you and to whom, how to meet people, shake hands, and on and on. Children are also learning how to care for themselves: dressing, tying shoes, eating, washing, bathing, brushing hair and teeth are among the many self-care skills children are learning at this age. Children are interested in learning to care for their home and family by making beds, cleaning, sweeping, cooking and gardening. These early practical skills strengthen social skills and relationships throughout our lives.

We can assist our children in acquiring skills by modeling and giving simple instructions. Allowing our children to watch and interact with us, as we work, models vital skills. We can also give short "lessons." For social skills, though, the teachable moment is not when we expect a certain behavior, but rather beforehand, with indirect preparation.

Perhaps neighbors are coming over for coffee. What social skills will your child need to be successful in this situation? Some of the social skills you might want to teach are greeting the neighbor, introducing oneself, offering a place to sit, offering food or drink, thanking guests for the visit, and saying goodbye. A short lesson for self-introduction might go like this:

"William, our neighbors are coming for coffee on Saturday. When they get here I'd like for you to introduce yourself. This is how you introduce yourself. Extend your hand and shake hands. Then say. "Hello. My name is William. I'm glad to meet you." Now let's pretend that I am Mr. or Ms. Jones. I'll walk through the door and you can practice greeting me."

Your child can practice with you several times before the visit. When the neighbors arrive, welcome them, and cue your child, by saying, "I'd like you to meet my son."

If William cannot remember what to do, forcing him to perform is not recommended. Just smile and go ahead and introduce him, knowing that some additional preparation is necessary. Remember, the teachable moment is not at the moment we are asking them to perform a new skill. Shyness, embarrassment, tiredness, and hunger can all contribute to an inability to perform a new skill, as we've all experienced.

To develop social skills, analyze what needs to be learned according to the situation and your child's behavior. Model with your own behavior and prepare your child indirectly with short lessons. In this way you can assist your child in acquiring social skills for a lifetime of successful relationships.

Understanding A Child's Sense of Order

Three-year-old Abby was the perfect cheerful morning preschool student with never a tear or a fret. Until the end of April. All week at dismissal she had begun to cry as soon as I opened the car door. Her mother was greeted with big sobs and screams of "You don't love me." Her mom was horrified and I was confused, to say the least.

Thursday morning during class I asked her why she was crying at dismissal.

"Because my momma doesn't love me anymore."

"Why do you think your momma doesn't love you anymore?"

"Because she took my blankie away."

A clue! I called Abby's mom and inquired about the blanket.

"Oh my gosh! It's gotten so warm that when I cleaned out the car last week, I washed it and put it away. Don't worry. I'm putting it in the car now."

When I opened the car door at dismissal, Abby let out a whoop of joy. "Momma, thank you for giving my blankie back. I love you!"

For Abby, life was not right unless her blankie was in her car. Her sense of order told her that her mom's love and the blanket had a connection. Not a logical thought, but Abby was in a sensitive period of development for order. This sensitive period is strongest from birth to age four-and-a-half.

Children are trying to create order out of chaos as they make their way out into the world. Language, movement, family relationships, and the ability to discern sensory information, all connect in the child's mind to create order and make sense of the world.

At this age, children learn by repetition by doing the same thing over and over, such as reading the same book, saying the same prayers, and singing the same songs. It is how they make order out of chaos. Around age six, with the loss of baby teeth, a more adult learning style develops where learning requires repetition but with variety. Until that time, though, children thrive on this stability in their environment. Children gain comfort, as well as expertise, in knowing the wooden blocks are in the same place, that the kitchen pans are in the lower left hand cabinet, and that lunch is at noon everyday.

The child's need for order may create seemingly outrageous demands. On his fifth birthday, Paul started to stay all day for the kindergarten program. After two days, he told his parents that he didn't want to come to school anymore, because he didn't like lunch.

"Paul," I asked, "what don't you like about lunch at school?"

His bottom lip almost touched the floor. "The food."

"What kind of food would you like at school?"

He went on to name three fast food places. He was in the habit of eating lunch out several times a week with his dad or mom. Lunch at school just didn't fit in with his established sense of order for lunch.

Paul learned to adjust, but not without a lot of complaining to his parents and teachers. We were able to work together, understanding that Paul's sense of order had been disturbed. Mom and Dad took turns coming to lunch at school a couple of times a week, and Paul learned to enjoy the food, different company and a new routine.

If your child is being difficult and moody, step back and reflect on what recent changes have occurred, remembering the importance of order in the young child. Many times moodiness stems from a change in routine or environment. It might be as simple as having washed the blankie.

Three Period Lessons Aid Sensory Development

Between the ages of birth to four-and-a-half, children are in a sensitive period for refining their senses. Children at this age are capable of learning to discern hundreds of qualities of the things around them. Perfect pitch is acquired before the age of six. Too often adults stop giving information after certain basics are mastered. Take the names of shapes. When a child can identify circle, square and triangle, we tend to stop. Keep going! Show the shapes and names of other figures such as oval, ellipse, quatrefoil, curvilinear triangle, rectangle, trapezoid, rhombus, quadrilateral, pentagon, hexagon, heptagon, octagon, nonagon and decagon.

We can do the same for solid figures: sphere, cube, pyramid, rectangular prism, cone, ellipsoid, ovoid, triangular prism, tetrahedron. Shapes and figures are just the beginning of the qualities we can show children. Colors, tastes, smells, dimension, materials and sounds are all sensory information that can be explored and named.

To introduce new information, isolating a quality of an object makes it easier to learn. Let's look at introducing the words for sphere, cube and pyramid. In an ideal situation the figures would be made of the same material, be the same color, and be on the same size scale. This would isolate the quality of shape. Using a green five-inch wooden cube, along with a red vinyl beach ball, and a one-inch tall white plastic pyramid will not isolate the unique quality of each figure. Instead, other qualities including size, color and material will be shown with the figure. Isolating one essential quality helps learning occur faster and with less confusion.

A few years ago I took an intensive language course in Spanish. How fast language sounds when you don't understand! Spanish words came at me so quickly, I had to ask simple questions such as, "Is this a green chair?" because I didn't understand which was more important, to get a chair or to get something green. I sympathize with three-year-olds. Fast and confusing language is directed at our children when so much is new. Isolating a quality took on a new importance for me when I was learning a new language.

To introduce new words, showing three things at a time seems to work well. Two items are not challenging enough and four can be too many. A Montessori teaching technique is the three period lesson. It goes like this:

First Period: Introduction

This is a circle. This is a square. This is a triangle.

Second Period: Show me.

Show me the triangle. Show me the square. Show me the circle.

We do many repetitions with the second period of the lesson, using a variety of expressions, such as: Put the circle in my hand. Place the triangle on the table. Carry the square to the chair.

Third Period: The Test

Point to the object and ask: What is this?

If the child knows it, add more information. If not, return to the second period of the lesson.

When working with children, remember that the main objective is to build a loving and trusting relationship. It is not about whether they can give you the right answer, right now. If a child tells you a square is a circle, avoid saying "No! That is a square!" Be friendly with error. Put your finger near the circle and then say, "Show me the circle." We want to assure success as we introduce new information to our children. It helps build trust and respect and thus true learning. Also, research shows that we remember new information best if it involves laughter. So have fun!

Sometimes we can do all three periods of the lesson in one session. Other times, it may be weeks between the first and third periods. Take clues from the look in your child's eyes. Three or four minutes per lesson are probably enough. Stop before your child becomes frustrated.

Learning sensory language can help your child cope more easily. If your child is a fussy eater or has temper tantrums, he or she may be on sensory overload. To analyze what triggers the behavior, begin by looking at your child's sensory environment. In the car, for example, music, engine noise, fabric textures, hot buckles, temperature changes, air circulation, smells or the inability to move may put a three-year-old, or any of us, on sensory overload before getting out of the driveway. Instead of kicking the seat and screaming, with acquired sensory language, your child may tell you, "Dad, the air conditioner is blowing into my eyes and freezing my eyeballs!"

Allowing Opportunities for Movement

A kid's got to move. Observing a few minutes at a playground will attest to that. You don't see children sitting around if they have the chance to run, jump, climb, or skip. Children are in a sensitive period of development for movement from birth to about age five-and-a-half.

Around age four-and-a-half, children have a growth spurt where their legs may grow over an inch per month. During this time, it is difficult for children to sit comfortably. They will squirm or refuse to sit in their chairs at the dinner table. They will appear to wander aimlessly about in their preschool classes. At this time, it is important to allow lots of opportunities for movement such as long walks and other outdoor activities.

Because of this leg growth, children need additional calcium. Many children suffer from leg cramps at night, don't sleep well and end up being very cranky. Be on the look out during this growth spurt. Children can't tell you about their legs cramps because they don't have the language experience in most cases. Additional calcium supplements, stretching and massage will help children (and parents!) get a good night's sleep, and restore pleasant dispositions.

Children love to walk on stonewalls, balance beams or lines drawn on the floor. At a playground observe all the different activities children do. Every movement is fulfilling a basic developmental need. Give your child opportunities to move and learn at the same time.

The need for movement, though, should not be a license to run wild in the house, stores, or restaurants. Purposeful activity needs to direct children's movement. We need to give activities that engage all the senses of the child and therefore help him or her direct energy for a positive outcome. For example, folding laundry is a purposeful activity. Children can fold laundry and make many trips to put the laundry away. Send them off with one towel to put away and have them come back and get the next one. It may take twenty trips, but they'll love it, especially when a big pile has disappeared.

You can also incorporate movement while sitting and waiting. The preposition game is a quiet game for a restaurant or doctor's appointment. It's simple to play with two objects. In a restaurant I'll use a napkin and spoon. Ask the child to do things such as: *Put the spoon under the napkin. Put the spoon next to the napkin. Put the napkin under the spoon. Put the spoon near the napkin. Put the napkin around the spoon.* Switch roles and let the child give you directions.

In a situation that allows more movement, use a book and table in the same manner. *Put the book under the table. Place the book near the table.* Change the prepositions using words such as over, above, near, through, far, around, between and for the more adventuresome, adjacent, tangent, perpendicular, horizontal, vertical, intersecting. Dig out that old geometry book! This game helps the child learn that certain words (prepositions) show the relationship between two or more objects. Have a good time and laugh at all the funny relationships you can describe for the objects. Each request is a walk across the room and directs movement in a purposeful manner.

A key to a happy child, and thus a happy parent, is using purposeful activities to allow movement that aids development. Household chores and word games give children purposeful movement. They'll have chances for movement along with learning responsibility for a cheerful home life.

Language Development is a Critical Stage from Birth to Six

From birth to six, children are in a critical period of language development, when the spoken word develops naturally. Ninety percent of our adult conversational language is in place by the age of six. If a child does not speak by age six, it is improbable that the child will acquire spoken, written or sign language beyond a two-year-old's comprehension level.

We don't have to teach children to walk or talk. Children thrive in an environment that encourages walking and talking during this critical stage of development. In normal development, a child will say his first word around twelve months and by thirty months will talk in sentences. When you are aware of your child's built-in developmental abilities, you can be of invaluable assistance by making sure your child's surroundings meet his developmental needs.

By thirty months of age, language is fully developed in the child. By thirty-six months, a child should be able to clearly speak in full sentences, with correct basic syntax (meaning words are spoken in meaningful order), and each sound in a word should be clear and intelligible. Unfortunately, for many children this is not the case. Ear infections, a long illness, separation from parents, physical or environmental challenges can cause language delays. Luckily, the critical period for language acquisition continues for another three years. At thirty-six months analyze your child's spoken language for areas that are weak and not fully developed. Once you recognize areas for language development, you can begin to enrich your child's learning in purposeful ways.

If you see speech difficulties, make sure that your child has no physical problems receiving or communicating information. Your pediatrician should be able to help you determine if vision, hearing, or muscle tone in the mouth and tongue are affecting language development. After addressing any physical challenges, you can begin to enrich your child's language environment and target specific skills.

Some of the most common language challenges that young children have are not pronouncing certain sounds clearly; mispronouncing words, such as *pasgetti* for spaghetti; using a sentence structure that omits certain parts of speech; or substituting a word like "thingy" or grunting when they don't know a word.

If your child is having difficulty making certain sounds, singing a simple song, using just one word over and over again is a good exercise. For example, if your child cannot say the "th" sound, sing "thank you" over and over again to the tune of "London Bridge is Falling Down." Sing the word "with" to work on the ending sound, and the word "without" for internal sound practice. Make it fun and silly and in a few days you will begin to see an improvement in your child's "th" sounds. If your child needs work with multiple sounds, concentrate on one at a time, adding one new sound per week while reviewing the previous ones.

To help with mispronounced words, be sure that everyone (siblings, grandparents, caregivers) speaks to your child using normal clear speech and does not use "baby talk." Some children's mispronounced words are cute and funny, but don't incorporate them into your speech. One of my difficult words to pronounce growing up was "yellow." My four younger siblings naturally mimicked my speech, and thought that the correct pronunciation for the color of the sun was "lellow." With my mother's patient efforts, we learned to pronounce it correctly. If she only had a nickel for every time she had to say yellow. Remember to use the correct word and no baby-talk.

If it doesn't sound cute on a thirty-year-old, don't let it be cute on a three-year-old.

Omitting pronouns and prepositions is another language challenge. If your child is saying things like "Me go play." kindly restate the sentence as "Yes, you are going to play outside." There is no need to force a child to repeat words or sentences after you. If your child sees and hears it the right way, he or she will soon be saying it correctly.

If you hear your child stumbling on finding the right word, do vocabulary enrichment using cards and simple naming of items in your home. Restate sentences with an appropriate word; "That handle thingy is called an umbrella." Reading out loud to your child every day will also help strengthen vocabulary along with listening skills.

To aid in your child's language development, be aware of how children naturally develop speech. Analyze your child's speaking skills at age three, focusing on enunciation, pronunciation, grammar and vocabulary skills. Keep language rich in your home and target specific skills. Then relax a little and let your child's natural ability to create language get to work.

Building Cathedrals Not Walls

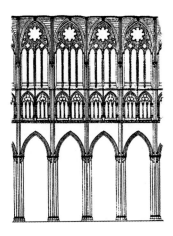

COLUMNS AND WALLS
Building Character

---

pon completion of the cathedral foundation, work began on the columns and walls. The six to eight feet thick columns, or piers, of a cathedral soar 200 to 300 or more feet high, basically 20 to 30 stories tall.

Stonemasons constructed the columns out of hundreds of pieces of cut stone. The cathedral columns were reinforced with iron as well as being cemented into place.

In comparison, our character is built from hundreds and thousands of daily experiences constructed on the strong and level foundation of family. Our character strengths are reinforced with love and experiences, the iron and concrete of life.

The cathedral columns alone were not strong enough to handle all the weight of the vault, or arched roofs, of the cathedral. The weight of the roof tended to push the walls outward. To take part of the strain and strengthen the walls, flying buttresses were connected to the columns. These flying buttresses transferred the stress back on to the foundation, allowing the walls to stand tall and true.

Scaffolding became necessary as the walls grew higher and higher. Work platforms were hoisted up the walls as long pieces of wood were expensive and scare. Stone steps and spiral staircases were built into the wall themselves to help gain access to the ever-higher platforms. Building columns was a dangerous and difficult job.

Creating conditions to create character strengths that last a lifetime and beyond requires skill and boldness.

Those with fear of heights need not apply.

Catch'em Doing Something Right

"All I do is tell Tim, 'no.' He's into everything and by the end of the day my fuse is short, and I lose it and yell. It hurts me to see the hurt in his eyes. But I'm just exhausted," Mary sighed over the phone to me.

Tim, a redheaded three-year-old, had been "busy" that day. He had opened a bag of flour all over the kitchen and dropped his plate of spaghetti while trying to clean up his spilled juice. In the bathtub he'd opened and emptied a new bottle of shampoo.

I knew Mary was going through a lot of transitions. With their recent move, she was home full-time. Her husband, Jeff, traveled overseas frequently and Mary was five months pregnant with their second child. I met Mary at a neighborhood party where we visited about her situation along with the frustration of not having a husband in the same time zone. When Mary discovered I was a teacher and had survived similar circumstances, she asked if she could call for "a sanity check." From personal experience, I know it is difficult to stay positive with many changes. From Mary's phone call, I sensed she wanted to see things differently.

"Mary," I asked, "what things did Tim do right today?"

"I know he must have done a lot of things perfectly," Mary replied. "I'm so frustrated I can't think of any."

"Let's look at when he got out of bed this morning," I said.

"Well, he got dressed by himself," Mary said.

"Okay. Great! Write that down. What did he do next?"

Mary told me Tim ate a good breakfast. He went cheerfully to preschool. He made a drawing for his grandparents. In a couple minutes, Mary came up with a list of seven things.

"Put that on the refrigerator," I suggested. "Then put a note in your pocket that says, *Catch him doing something right.* Carry it all week and when you see Tim doing something right, tell him, right then. Don't gush. Just state the facts. For example: I see you ate a nice breakfast. I like how you are ready for school. I enjoy cooking with you. Try to ignore and make light of any mishaps. Be friendly with error. Remember, he's learning. At bedtime, tell him the story of his day with all the tasks that he did well. Also ask him what was wonderful about his day. Try it for a week and see if it helps."

"I think I can do that. Timothy is a great little guy and I think this will help me remember it even if I'm tired," Mary said.

As Mary related the "trouble" that Timothy had caused, I recognized the incidents as motivated by a desire to help. Like most three-year-olds, Timothy had the attitude for success, just not the skills. Working with young children for many years, I see how they want to please but lack the inner discipline and skill level to match actions with intentions. They have the will but not the skill. To develop skills we need to give opportunities to work and make mistakes in a friendly environment. Because their memory and skill level are developing, children can do something one day and not the next. When we focus on positive behavior, we'll reinforce skills, attitude and long-term memory.

A week or so later, I saw Mary at the grocery. She felt that focusing on what Tim was doing right and being friendly with error was helping her stay calm, and Tim seemed to be less work.

"Tim told me at bedtime that his 'favorite thing' was having a happy mom. Jeff could see the difference, too, when he got back home. He asked me what I was doing with Tim," Mary said with a laugh, "and I told him. Just catching him doing something right!"

Using Positive Statements With Children

"If I tell Ginny not to do something, she just looks me in the eye, and does it. She seems defiant," Sam, Ginny's dad, told me at a company picnic.

Ginny, an almost four-year-old curly headed brunette, ran over from the swings at the park. "Ginny, how about playing a little game with me? I'm going to ask you to do some things like sit, stand on one leg, or smile. Are you ready?"

Ginny eagerly awaited my instructions. She perfectly followed my commands to sit, walk, jump, hop on one leg, bend over, blink her eyes, pat her head, clap her hands and more.

I threw in a negative command. "Don't jump." Ginny looked at me with big eyes and…jumped, followed by a grimace.

I returned to giving positive commands. She again followed all my commands. Then I said, "Don't smile." Her eyebrows went up. She smiled and squealed, "I can't do it!"

I laughed with her and said, "Yes, the don'ts are hard to do."

As Ginny ran back to the swings, I asked Sam if he had seen what happened.

"Well, it looked like she just couldn't keep herself from jumping or smiling when you told her not to do those things," Sam said.

"Did you see a defiant look on her face?" I said.

"Before, I thought it was defiance. Now I know it's confusion. Why is that?"

"Until about age seven, the brain hasn't developed enough to understand what don't means and have rest of the body act on it. 'Don't jump' actually means 'do anything but jump.' Life experience tells us it means, 'stand still.' It takes a lot of language experience to correctly react to a negative command."

"How can I change what I say to Ginny so she understands better?" Sam asked.

I told Sam that I could give him a list of positive statements. Also, I cautioned him that it takes a while to change our language patterns because we are so used to saying things like "Don't run" instead of "walk." From what I've observed in children, changing is worth the effort.

"Sam," I continued "once you get used to stating commands in the positive, you'll find that you are clearer and more explicit in your instructions to everyone."

One mom, who took the time to use the following list, said her performance review at work highlighted her "ability to state things in a clear and positive manner." Not only had her child benefited, her co-workers had too.

Use this list, along with modeling desired behavior, to help your child learn to "do the don'ts."

A short list of positive statements:

Don't talk.	Please be quiet.
Don't run.	Walk.
Don't go that way.	Come here. Stay with me.
Don't touch.	Put your hands behind your back.
Don't forget.	Remember your jacket.
Don't wiggle.	Sit like this.
Don't play with food.	Use your fork.
Don't throw that.	Stop. Put it down. Hand me that.
Don't play the TV loud.	Make the TV quieter.
Don't yell.	Speak softly. Use an inside voice.
Don't hit.	Use your words.
Don't make a face.	Smile.

To make statements more positive, add please and thank you!

Understanding the Three Hour Work Cycle

Tired and agitated, Sara got ready for bed. What had happened to the day? She had woken up fresh that morning, ready to have a productive day.

During breakfast, Sara's assistant called to alert Sara that she wouldn't be in to copy the reports for the next day's meeting. When Sara went to make copies of her presentation, the toner cartridge was low, the paper jammed and the machine ran out of staples. When Sara reviewed her copies, page 17 was missing. Sara's lunch appointment cancelled while Sara was waiting in the restaurant. After lunch, she couldn't get on-line to do some research. Then Ron, a co-worker, came in and complained about his weekend for half an hour. What went wrong with Sara's day? Sara was unable to get a work cycle completed.

A work cycle consists of selecting an activity, doing it, achieving some internal satisfaction for the work, then selecting the next task.

When we experience this cycle of "choose-do-return to order-satisfaction, then choose again," we create a powerful success cycle with feelings of accomplishment and contentment.

When we are having a productive work cycle, we'll say we are "on a roll." We go from task to task, choosing progressively harder tasks as time allows. On those high achieving days, we feel unstoppable.

Then there are the days when we get off to fits and starts because we are interrupted, don't have enough time to complete a task before another commitment, or we lack the necessary supplies. How that trip to the hardware store can sabotage the best efforts for a productive workday.

Most of us, even small children, have a built in three-hour work cycle. We might contrast and compare it to our sleep cycle. When we know we have at least three hours of uninterrupted time, we will tackle a multitude of jobs and enjoy doing it. If our time is interrupted, we may not even try to start anything. "It's not worth the effort, or I don't feel like doing anything," we might say. Sound familiar?

When given a regular three-hour period, children (and adults) learn to tap into a success cycle. After accomplishing a series of short and familiar tasks in a ninety minute time frame, a child will choose a task that is challenging and represents "true learning." At this ninety-minute mark there is a period of restlessness that lasts about ten minutes, until the choice for the challenging activity is made. The new activity may last for sixty to ninety minutes.

Here's an example of a recent Saturday morning three-hour work cycle for me. Not very glamorous but I was on a roll.

Clean kitchen, 15 minutes. Start laundry, 15 minutes. Make phone calls for appointments, 20 minutes. Vacuum, 20 minutes. Feeling of restlessness, What should I do next? Cup of coffee, 10 minutes. Balance bank statements and pay bills, 90 minutes.

Here's an example of a four-and-a-half-year-old's work cycle that I recently observed. Work puzzle, 10 minutes. Build with blocks, 15 minutes. Water plants, 20 minutes. Sweep floor, 10 minutes. Number counting cards, 15 minutes. Walk up and down steps, 5 minutes. Talk with dad, 10 minutes. Do 100 piece puzzle, 45 minutes. Practice tying shoes, 45 minutes.

When we have achieved a three-hour work cycle, normally we are eager to begin the next cycle. Productive adults have two to four work cycles a day. Children under the age of five usually have one work cycle a day. Around five, children will start a second work cycle if given the opportunity.

The gift of uninterrupted time gives us, children and adults, the opportunity to engage in our own powerful three-hour work cycles, creating personal success in learning, concentration and independence.

Independence and Concentration

"Concentration and distractibility are particular sensitive indicators of a variety of conditions affecting children. Highly concentrated activity suggests that the child's finding satisfaction and challenge in a task. Distractibility suggests trouble of some kind, social, psychological or whatnot." — Jerome Bruner, Under Five in Britain

Zach began the 18th hole of miniature golf. Twelve-year-old Zach was ahead, and one under par. A wager of a pizza with my husband was in the balance. Zach stayed focused and won the match by two strokes.

There should have been fireworks. The band should have played a Sousa march. The mayor should have presented Zach with keys to the city. Why?

Because I had finally observed Zach having concentration and independence, two traits needed to be a fully functioning person. I say finally observed, since I have known Zach since he was six years old and in my classroom. To say he was motivated to do school work would be an understatement. Zach needed constant supervision and encouragement to finish simple tasks. It would take him all day to finish six math problems, or write ten sentences. A mule stuck in the mud would have shown more independence and concentration than Zach.

Now I witnessed the independence and concentration that would serve him well for rest of his life. I was elated. Overjoyed.

Children who are having trouble developing independence and focus in their activities usually drive the adults around them to distraction. These children though, need to be directed to activities that hold their interest and attention. (Sorry, television, computer and video games don't count.) From a glimmer of interest and attention, concentration builds. Zach showed interest in singing, doing plays, designing props, drawing, gardening, fossils and animals, so I tried to incorporate these interests into his academic work. Pure academic work did not hold his interest.

Five-year-old Bradley had begun to read short phonetic words. After spring break, he returned to the classroom unable to sound out the words he had known two weeks previously. Trying to coax him into reading activities was met with a firm "No, thank you," as he continued to cut strips of paper from our scissor cutting lesson. His first day back, Bradley cut strips of paper all day long. At clean up, Bradley asked if he could take some paper home.

"Fine," I agreed, hoping that his mother didn't ask me what he had done all day.

The next day, Bradley cut paper strips in the morning and afternoon sessions. Day Three, I visited with his mom. "I've never had a student do an activity like this for three days straight. I'm not sure what to think, but as long as he's showing concentration, I'd like not to intervene."

Bradley's mom nodded. "He's come home and cut for at least two hours. Surely, he'll want to do something else soon."

At Day Ten, Bradley had cut through every cutting exercise paper we had. He had cut straight lines, curved lines, zigzag lines, and spirals.

Day Eleven Bradley entered the classroom, and selected a reading exercise. Bradley spent the next six weeks involved in reading and writing exercises with not a pair of scissors in sight.

What I learned from Bradley was this: If you observe children doing purposeful activity independently and with concentration, let them be. Observe, and know that they are headed in the right direction, even though the work might not be what you would choose for them to do.

If we allow our children to listen and follow their inner teacher, whether it is playing miniature golf, or cutting strips of paper, we can be assured that the independence and concentration from one activity will be transferred to subsequent activities of interest.

As I watched Zach calmly and coolly birdie that last hole and when I heard Bradley read hippopotamus, I knew that their concentrated and independent activities in non-academic work had served them well.

The Positive Psychology of Childhood

"The families I see day in and day out come to me to fix problems. If they had done some preparation before becoming parents, a lot of pain could have been avoided," said Debra, a family psychologist. "It's much more fun and rewarding to help people learn to create happy families from the beginning, instead of trying to help after something blows up in their faces."

Debra was talking about using positive psychology to create optimum situations for personal growth. As parents we are in a unique position to help our children learn to be happy, healthy and maintain a positive outlook on life.

The innate nature of the child is to be happy and we are all born with natural tendencies that aid personal development. We are born with dispositions to love and connect with the adults in our lives, to love our surroundings, and to love the natural world. Even a newborn has the inclination toward activity directed by an individual will, a will that constructs a unique human being.

The newborn comes prepared to create a happy life, but obstacles get in the way. Uninformed or misinformed adults for the most part create these impediments to personal development.

Psychology has been dedicated to understanding mental illness. Positive psychology seeks to understand the factors that create happy and healthy "mindedness."

Positive psychologists have identified six types of core virtues that appear in all cultures—wisdom and knowledge, courage, humanity, justice, temperance, transcendence—comprised of twenty-four character strengths:

1. *Wisdom and Knowledge*: creativity, curiosity, open-mindedness, love of learning, perspective

2. *Courage*: bravery, persistence, integrity, vitality

3. *Humanity*: love, kindness, social intelligence

4. *Justice*: citizenship, fairness, leadership

5. *Temperance*: forgiveness and mercy, humility and modesty, prudence and self-regulation

6. *Transcendence*: appreciation of beauty and excellence, gratitude, hope, humor and spirituality

Debra wanted to help individuals and families understand these 24 character strengths in order to build healthy lives. Knowing our strengths can help us be more engaged in life, find deeper meaning, have higher aspirations, feel more satisfied and even laugh and smile more often, regardless of our circumstances. Being able to identify our strengths and learn how to use them can help us fortify our families, our communities, and ourselves. This knowledge creates a foundation for sustaining a positive outlook on life and a resiliency against life's difficulties.

The Positive Psychology Center at the University of Pennsylvania has an on-line testing site to assess these 24 strengths in adults and children. Go to www.authentichappiness.com and take the VIA (Virtues in Action) Signature Strengths Questionnaire to assess character strengths. For children, use the VIA Strength Survey for Children.

Strengthen your strengths and bolster your weaknesses. This is an effective strategy for teaching your children how to use their natural positive tendencies, and will help all of us play to our positive qualities. Character strengths will create these six virtues that lead to a lifetime of well being.

Let's examine each of these virtues in the next essays.

Teaching Wisdom and Knowledge

Wisdom and knowledge. Some people mistakenly use these terms interchangeably. Knowledge is the state of familiarity, awareness, or understanding gained through experience or study. We know something because we have taken information in through our senses or mind.

Wisdom is the ability to discern or judge what is true, right, or lasting. Wisdom is common sense and good judgment. In the words of Henry David Thoreau, "It is a characteristic of wisdom not to do desperate things."

In positive psychology, wisdom and knowledge are defined by five character strengths—creativity, curiosity, open-mindedness, love of learning, and perspective. When we can observe these strengths in a person, we know that the virtues of wisdom and knowledge are being served.

How do we help develop these strengths?

We prepare an environment where self-directed exploration and activity are encouraged. How many companies in the U.S.A were started by garage inventors? Wisdom and knowledge are nourished with the freedom to explore and try new and different things.

We want a place that arouses curiosity. Reading *Little Women* I came across the term medicinal leeches. Asking my mother, she simply said, "Oh, I can't tell you at the dinner table. It's too gruesome." Boy, did that get my curiosity going all the way to the encyclopedia.

We need to nurture creativity. Thomas Edison labored years to design the incandescent light bulb. Of his work Edison remarked:

> *Results? Why, man, I have gotten lots of results! If I find 10,000 ways something won't work, I haven't failed. I am not discouraged, because every wrong attempt discarded is often a step forward...*

To nurture creativity, we need to allow exploration and failure as important learning and strength building activities.

We need to model open-mindedness. A friend of mine brought up in France loves to take the opposite point of view in a discussion. At first I thought she was argumentative until I came across an article that explained how the French educational system encourages debate and discussion on every topic. The favorite pastime in France is to analyze and discuss a subject from all angles. For Americans that method may not seem practical, efficient or necessary. Being able to articulate a perspective other than your own nourishes an open and curious mind. Another friend seems to answer any suggestion with "Why not?" His question creates an opening to gain a fresh insight into an issue.

We need to foster a love of learning. A buzzword in schools today is "life-long learners." People who are open to growth and change give themselves high ratings on the happiness scale. Happiness in this case was defined as feeling that you are being and acting your true self. When we are creative, curious, and open-minded, being open to learning seems to be a natural development.

We need to develop multiple perspectives about our lives. We need to develop the art of the long view, along with short-term strategies. We need to marvel at the scene under the microscope and be overwhelmed with the constellations. As we survey the world from small to large, present to past, and back again, perhaps we can begin to understand how our situation fits in the overall picture of humanity.

Knowledge and wisdom expand in the world when we provide opportunities for our children, our families and our communities to be curious, creative, open-minded, excited about learning, and have perspective. With knowledge and wisdom, peace follows. Why not?

Teaching Courage

Courage incorporates four character strengths—bravery, persistence, integrity and vitality. Courage is the state or quality of mind or spirit that enables one to face danger, fear, or difficulties with self-possession, confidence and resolution.

How do we help our children develop these strengths that are called courage?

Bravery is the ability to do what you think is right even if it risks personal injury or sacrifice. Our Founding Fathers exhibited bravery by signing the Declaration of Independence, knowing that the ink at the bottom of the page was a death warrant for treason against the British Crown.

Most of us don't have to "pledge to each other our Lives, our Fortunes and our sacred Honor." Being brave means being true to yourself. The phrase, "Sei brav" in German translates literally as "be good." When we are brave, we are good to ourselves by facing our fears and living our dreams. Everyday we practice bravery by living our lives in a manner that reflects our values, character, and aspirations.

Persistence is the ability to get up from being knocked down one more time than anybody else. It is the ability to hold firmly and steadfastly to a purpose or undertaking despite obstacles, warnings, or setbacks. Does it sound a lot like bravery and being true to yourself?

Calvin Coolidge had something to say about persistence:

> *"Nothing in this world can take the place of persistence. Talent will not; nothing is more common than unsuccessful people with talent. Genius will not; unrewarded genius is almost a proverb. Education will not; the world is full of educated derelicts. Persistence and determination alone are omnipotent. The slogan "press on" has solved and always will solve the problems of the human race."*

Integrity comes from the word *integer* meaning whole. We have integrity when what we say and do is in synch with our personal beliefs and values. People with integrity "walk their talk." People with integrity take personal responsibility for their lives and don't blame others for disappointments or obstacles. People with integrity feel whole because they possess self-awareness while connecting to a higher purpose.

Vitality. People with vitality bring enthusiasm and energy to whatever task they are doing, however trivial. Vital people exude positive expectations. Growth and challenge cannot flourish in an overprotected environment. A person with vitality is more concerned with growth and development than perfectionism.

To strengthen bravery, persistence, integrity and vitality in our children, we must turn discouragement into encouragement in four critical ways.

1. We have to show confidence in our children's abilities by giving them responsibility, asking for their opinions or advice, and avoiding the temptation to over-protect or rescue them from difficulties.

2. We need to focus on our children's strengths by acknowledging what they do well, by redirecting strengths to positive outcomes, by concentrating on improvement versus perfection, and by coaching and cheering as progress is made. Encouragement always works better than fear to help a child maintain focus on a goal.

3. Value each child as a unique person, a person who is on a personal schedule of development. We need to separate personal worth from accomplishments and mistakes.

4. Encourage independence by helping your child learn to do things for him or herself. It is being independent that develops confidence and leads to interdependence with others.

How to develop courage is simple. Encourage your child.

Teaching Humanity

The core virtue of humanity is comprised of the character strengths of love, kindness and social intelligence.

Humanity is the ability to see the connectedness of all human beings; it is the ability to help and befriend others.

One of the gifts of human beings is our ability to love. We love our families. We love our friends. We love our community, our nation, and our world. It is love that motivates us to help others, to design, to create, and serve other people. The ability to love and use love to meet others needs is a distinctly human attribute.

Kindness involves doing good deeds to help other people. With kindness, we take care of other people, thinking of their comfort and needs, possibly before our own. Kindness as a strength makes us generous and compassionate towards others. People who have this personal attribute have discovered that in the long term it is more productive to be kind than right. People with kindness as a strength have discovered that with kindness you can change the heart of an issue in a way that debating or fighting never can.

William Wordsworth, the English poet (1770-1850) wrote,
"That best portion of a good man's life,
His little, nameless, unremembered acts of kindness and of love."

It is the little kindnesses that are remembered and stored in the heart and mind. Kindness is the stuff that makes us human and defines our humanity.

Social intelligence comes into play in the growth of our humanity. To be socially intelligent we have to be aware of our own motives and emotions, as well as knowing about the feelings and desires of others. We need to be socially flexible, by realizing what to do in different social circumstances. Being socially aware and being positively engaged with others creates a well being in us. Positive engagement helps us express love and kindness as well as places value on close relations with others.

When psychologists studied the top ten percent of people who rated themselves as "very happy" they found that those people spent the least time alone and the most time socializing. The fewer the number of social contacts a person has, the greater the risk for depression and ill health.

When we can express our humanity through love, kindness and positive interaction with other people, we become happier, healthier and better humans.

One might see the research as indicating that we need to practice certain skills everyday to develop our humanity. Express our love and concern for others. Do kind deeds. Interact positively with other people.

When we can help our children learn to turn their random acts of kindness into intentional acts of kindness, perhaps true humanity will flourish.

Teaching Justice

Justice is comprised of the character strengths of citizenship, fairness and leadership. Vibrant community life is dependent on the civic strengths and skills of its members.

The job of citizenship brings with it a need for social responsibility, loyalty and teamwork. A friend, a new American citizen, wrote, "I am determined in helping this country become as great as it should be according to the morals established in its constitution." Would that all of us could have this attitude of loyalty, obligation and teamwork towards the good of all people.

To be strong citizens we need to have robust interpersonal skills. We need to be able to work well as part of a team or as a member of a group. We need to do our share and not say, "That's somebody else's job." We need to participate in the goal setting and objectives of our groups, and work to see that the agreed upon ideas become physical reality despite whatever difficulties occur. Loyal derives from the words *legal* and *law*, which in turn mean, "that which is laid down." The idea of citizenship originated with the concept that we come together as a group and decide what we need to do for the common good, and then pledge our part, our loyalty, to make it happen.

Fairness is part of justice. Fair, with its roots in Old English words for lovely and pleasant, connotes that when problems are solved fairly the situation turns out pleasant for all involved. To help make difficulties "lovely," though, takes a dispassionate and objective mind to determine how to handle conflict in a manner that is consistent with a group's rules, logic and ethics. Sorting through the issue to determine fairness to all concerned is usually not considered a pleasant or "fair" task. Being fair, however, is an essential component of the civic strengths that create justice.

Leadership skills determine the level of justice in a community. Strong leaders know how to encourage others to get important tasks completed. At this same time, strong leaders manage and maintain good relationships and respect within the organization. Strong leaders recognize problems readily and address each issue by organizing their group to discuss and remedy the situation. Strong leaders have the determination to see these solutions to fulfillment.

Skills in citizenship, fairness and leadership all begin at home. Family is where we first practice working with others, being loyal to a group and doing one's share. It is in our families that we begin to learn about making situations fair and pleasant to everyone in the group. It is in our homes that we model and learn leadership by encouraging each family member to do tasks important to the group, by maintaining good relations within the group, and by organizing group activities and making sure that they occur.

If we want to see justice in the world, we need to realize it begins at home.

Teaching Temperance

Personal strengths that protect against excess comprise the idea of temperance. Studies by positive psychologists indicate that strengths in forgiveness and mercy, humility and modesty, prudence, and self-regulation help us temper our thoughts and actions.

Mohandas Gandhi lived a life of temperance. Gandhi gave us the example of how temperance is a way to change the world. The study of his life can show us ways to strengthen our own character to avoid the excesses that would create a life of unhappiness.

Being able to show forgiveness and mercy to others when you have been dealt with badly shows strength of character. It takes a strong person to forgive a misdeed and not fall into the trap of revenge. It takes strength to accept the shortcomings of others. It takes confidence of your strength to give people a second chance when they have fallen short of expectations. As Gandhi said about seeking revenge, "An eye for an eye only ends up making the whole world blind."

Letting one's accomplishments speak for themselves, seeking the worth of every person, and being able to see each person's uniqueness in the grand scheme are the attributes of humility and modesty. To be humble and modest in today's jargon seem to mean being easily imposed on or submissive. True humility and modesty are terms used for servant leadership. In effective leadership, you lead by showing patience, and gentility in helping others, even though you may be better educated, or wealthier than those around you. Humility and modesty show a character strength that is at the core of leaders.

Being attentive to possible hazards or risks and planning for the future are the fruits of being prudent. The word prudence comes from the word *providence,* meaning to plan ahead or having foresight. Today calling someone a prude is a derogatory term instead of referring to a woman of strength and foresight. The strength of having prudence is that one is careful about one's choices, doesn't take unnecessary risks, and avoids saying or doing things that might cause hardship to oneself or others later.

Exhibiting control over one's emotions, thoughts and actions is another distinguishing characteristic of temperance. Learning to control one's moods and appetites becomes inner strength. Being able to make yourself do something you might not want to do, while knowing that in the end it is the best course of action, is the hallmark of inner or self-discipline. Being able to self-regulate gives us the ability to meet our goals and objectives in life.

Gandhi told us, "You must be the change you seek in the world."

If we want to help our children to have character strengths to live in a world where life is not lived an eye for an eye, we must model the self-control, the foresight, the servant leadership and the forgiveness we seek in the world.

Teaching Transcendence

Transcendence refers to the universal virtue that consists of the ability to express an appreciation of beauty and excellence, gratitude, hope, humor, and spirituality.

The virtue of transcendence helps us create connections to everything in the universe. These connections in turn help us create meaning and understanding in our lives. William Blake in his "Auguries of Innocence" wrote,

To see a World in a Grain of Sand

And a Heaven in a Wild Flower,
Hold Infinity in the palm of your hand
And Eternity in an hour.

It is the power of transcendence that helps us connect a grain of sand to eternity. With our observations and understanding we begin to notice beauty and appreciate excellence in all aspects of the world.

No matter how modest our circumstances, we can learn to see the beauty that surrounds us. It is this ability to see the wonder filled, the awe inspiring and the miraculous that helps give our life meaning and sustenance.

Developing an attitude of gratitude creates another character strength. Being thankful for our lives, the people in our lives, our experiences, our comforts, and even our tough times creates a resiliency in our character. This resiliency sustains us during the times that our lives on this planet are not going as expected. Taking time to express thanks to those around you and to a higher power will develop an inner strength that is not easily diminished.

The ability to laugh and make others laugh, to see the humor in a situation, to see the sunny side of the street when walking in the shadows, these are skills that keep us from being swallowed by self-pity. If human beings couldn't laugh, the universe would be sucked into a black hole. Cultivating a sense of humor, as they say, is the best medicine.

Hope and optimism are habits we all should practice and learn. Believing and working everyday to better ourselves and our world creates a life-affirming positive attitude that is difficult to extinguish no matter the hardship. As an old English adage says, "Hope for the best. Prepare for the worst. And be happy with whatever you get."

The character strength of spirituality, or holding beliefs about having a higher purpose in the scope of the universe, creates success and inner peace. Hallmarks of happy and resilient people are the ability to feel a connection with a higher power, along with having beliefs about the meaning of life that shape conduct and provide comfort.

As we nurture our children let us remember to stop and appreciate the beauty that surrounds us. Let's help children learn to show thanks for their lives and everything in it. Let's teach them how to laugh at themselves and to see the humor in a situation. Let us show our children that we are spiritual beings having a human experience. Last, but not least, when times get tough, let's display a spirit of hope and optimism, by pointing the way to the future to our children.

Three Gifts

From birth we are given at least three gifts to create positive change in our lives. When these gifts are nurtured we can become the creative force in our own lives. The gifts allow us to become the writer, the director and the actor in the production called "Our Life."

Choice. From the beginning, choice is a part of our human make-up. It is this innate ability to choose that leads us to positive growth and happiness. Between stimulus, what happens to us, and response, how we act, there is a space. Contained in that space is our freedom and our power to choose our response to any circumstance.

The more we practice choosing, the more confident we become in our ability to make positive decisions that lead to a life well-lived. Having the ability to choose is given to us, and we always have a choice for our response. We strengthen our skill by exercising our gift of being able to choose. It is with our choices that we write the script for our life.

Natural laws and universal principles. The natural laws and universal principles that govern our lives are another present given to us. These laws and principles direct our lives whether we are aware of them or not.

There are physical laws, such as, gravity, the rotation of the earth, and the earth's motion around the sun, to name only a few. Principles of human behavior, such as kindness, respect, honesty, personal integrity, and service to mankind, operate constantly in every culture on our planet.

Physical laws guide our actions because we cannot change the forces that are exerted on us. We choose to ignore the force of gravity at our own peril. We can't stop day turning into night, or the earth from moving through the universe. Physical laws control the consequences of our physical choices.

Likewise, we ignore universal principles with dangerous results. Choosing to use principles, such as respect, kindness and trust, enables us to tap into a moral authority to guide our lives through many hazards. If we choose to make decisions and place value in our life on activities not based on universal principles that are self-evident, factual, objective and impersonal, well, we will have a hard row to hoe.

Universal principles direct our lives with objective cause and effect. Disregard principles of human behavior and the effects can seem very personal and subjective. When we are cognizant of these underlying principles of life, we are more likely to make wise choices.

Inborn intelligence. Our third gift is ourselves; our bodies, our hearts, our minds and our spirits. We might say we are comprised of four distinct intelligences: physical, social/emotional, mental and spiritual. How we choose to use our talents depends on the tools, people, ideas, and natural surroundings in which we find ourselves. Our intelligences allow us to act on our choices and principles.

Each of us is given three gifts: choice, physical and spiritual laws that are objective, factual, impersonal, and self-evident, along with the innate intelligence to act on our choices and values. As adults, let us recognize and use these natural endowments to help our children and as well as ourselves.

Understanding Happiness

Happy. In our culture we use this word as though happy is a goal unto itself. An elusive objective, indeed.

The meanings of happiness and pleasure are used interchangeably in our world. Happiness and pleasure are not the same concept and to think so is dangerous. Pleasure seeking will not bring us happiness. Conversely, happiness is rarely found in pleasant activities, or activities designed to avoid pain or hardship.

In the dictionary, the word "happy" has sparse company along with its root word, *hap*, meaning luck, fortune, chance or an occurrence. Happiness, happen, hapless, haply, happenstance are happy's only companions. From its original Old English roots, happy relates to having good luck or fortune.

Our American idea of "the pursuit of happiness" pertains to the right to participate in activities that bring us good fortune. It is about the right to keep our life moving in a positive direction. Our forefathers saw the "pursuit of happiness" as an unalienable right. We have the right, and the corresponding responsibility, to take advantage of the circumstances that "happen" to come our way. We have the right to make events happen in our lives. We have the right to search for our luck, or as we say nowadays, follow our bliss.

As we go after the "hap" in our lives, it is not guaranteed to be pleasurable. As we follow our bliss in the pursuit of happiness, we are energized as we work in the direction of our dreams. When we are fully engaged in activities that are purposeful to our pursuit of happiness, we experience a feeling of being connected to something larger than ourselves. Obstacles and hardships are endured and overcome as part of the journey.

These experiences of being fully engaged create happiness. The completion of a meaningful task brings us pleasure and confidence to choose the next thing to "happen" to us. In the words of Thoreau, "Go confidently in the direction of your dreams. Live the life you've imagined."

True pleasure is the end product of choosing activities and successfully completing tasks that give meaning to our lives. Trying to recreate this "natural high" feeling of satisfaction and purpose without the corresponding activity or work can create addictive behaviors. The abuse of alcohol, drugs, sex, or food to simulate satisfaction can tragically lead to a downward spiral of pleasure seeking that separates a person from the ability to choose what "happens" in his or her life. Addictive behavior ultimately destroys a person's ability to pursue happiness.

What does this pursuit of happiness mean to us as we work with our children?

We need to help our children learn that positively participating in their lives by making choices and taking full responsibility for those choices is the path to happiness. We need to help our children see the "hap" or luck inherent in each situation, and help our children learn to have the skills and confidence to follow those opportunities.

Let's show our children that it is not the pursuit of pleasure but the enthusiastic participation in activities that fully engage us that brings enduring happiness. Happiness is not about feeling good all the time. It is about choosing to do good with the opportunities we happen to have. Happiness is about having the right and the responsibility to make life happen.

Build Relationships with Frequent Deposits

Relationship building is work, and our relationships and the trust in those relationships are in constant change. We maintain and deepen our relationships with regular acts of kindness, consideration, appreciation and service.

Every act of building relationship is as if we are making a deposit into a savings account. We increase our balance by giving a person a compliment, a kind word, or doing a thoughtful deed.

We deplete our relationship accruals by trying to manipulate others, being unkind or discourteous, breaking promises, being self-serving, lying, and holding grudges, to name a few types of "withdrawals." When we let our ego, arrogance, pride, impatience, need for control, self-centeredness, and need to be right become more important than the other person, we'll find ourselves confronted with a severely overdrawn relationship balance. We can bankrupt the relationship by taking more out of the relationship than we put in.

To maintain a healthy relationship we need to make regular and frequent deposits, preferably daily (that daily interest adds up quickly) into our relationship accounts.

How can we make deposits? ASK. Appreciation. Service. Kindness. Ask yourself, and the other person in the relationship, these questions: What can I do to show you that I appreciate you? How can I serve to enrich your life? How can I show you kindness?

Children might have a hard time telling us how they want to be appreciated, how to enrich their lives, and how to show them kindnesses, but ask anyway. You might get some interesting and valuable feedback.

A preschool class discussion about acts of kindness yielded some of these responses:

A five-year-old student said she knew her father loved her because he always put the peanut butter up to the very edge of her sandwich.

A three-year-old said his night-light from his grandmother made him feel loved.

A four-year-old girl said going to get an ice cream cone with her dad, by herself, was her favorite thing to do.

When asked what they did to make others feel loved, some answers follow:

I eat my spaghetti without crying.

I put my pajamas on by myself.

I kiss my momma.

I help my sister when she falls down.

I say "peas" and "tank you."

It is in our daily acts of appreciation, service and kindness that our relationships grow and the dividends multiply.

Ask your children two questions: What do I do that makes you feel loved? What do you do to make me feel loved?

Expect accelerated compound interest in a terrific investment.

Building Cathedrals Not Walls

FLYING BUTTRESSES
The Art of Parenting

---

 o build the flying buttresses, workers constructed temporary wooden frames that supported the walls until the buttresses could be built and the mortar thoroughly cured.

To take part of the strain and strengthen the walls, flying buttresses were connected to the columns. These flying buttresses transferred the stress back on to the foundation, allowing the walls to stand tall and true.

The art of parenting supports the building of character strengths in our children. As we are learning to be parents, or becoming flying buttresses to support our children's character development, we need to be supported by the temporary framework of our own parents and other caring adults in our community.

It is our job as adults to support the development of our children. When our foundation is solid, and our framework is sure, the stresses of the job can be easily supported by a well-built foundation of love, family and work.

Be Proactive And Choose How You'll Parent

"If I have to go to another staff meeting and hear about being proactive, I might react negatively," Ann said as she took off her coat at the coffee shop. "Enough about me. Tell me what you've been writing."

I laughed. Ann probably didn't want to hear about this column, but her comments strengthened my desire to write about the importance of being proactive, the first habit of Stephen Covey's *Seven Habits of Highly Effective People*.

A fundamental principle of being human, Covey tells us, is this: Between stimulus and response, we have the freedom to choose. How we choose is a combination of our levels of self-awareness, imagination, conscience and independent will.

When we have the habit of being proactive, we become responsible for our lives and our situation, along with making decisions based on principles and reflection. To be highly effective in our parenting roles, we need to be in the habit of acting proactively, even, if like my friend Ann, we are weary of hearing about it.

The idea of having the freedom to choose our response, no matter the circumstance, is fundamental to being proactive. Becoming self-aware of our language can help us develop a habit of being in control and not reacting to our problems. Becoming aware of reactive language, then using our imagination, independent will and conscience to view problems differently will create new habits. If we find ourselves saying, "There's nothing I can do," we need to stop and change it to "Let's look at different alternatives." We can turn, "He makes me so mad" into "I can choose how I respond."

Josie, stepmother to four-year old Pete, told me, "Pete drives me crazy. He's loud. He's rude. He's messy. He's destructive. He took scissors to the upholstery on our new couch."

"Why," I asked, "do you choose to let Pete drive you crazy?"

Josie shot me an angry look. "What do you mean, I choose to let him drive me crazy?"

"Just that. I think you can change this situation, by choosing to think differently about Pete and stepping back and using your imagination."

"What we feeds grows. If you are concentrating on the behaviors that drive you crazy, then Pete's misbehavior becomes a self-fulfilling prophecy as you look for more behavior to 'drive you crazy.'"

"I should look for behavior that doesn't drive me crazy and not react to the stuff that bothers me?" Josie said, eyebrows arching.

"Think of it as backwards thinking or trying to look at a situation with imagination and humor. I think as soon as you realize you are the adult-in-charge, and you choose to let a four-year-old boy and his behavior 'drive you sane,' you'll be a more effective parent. And a lot happier."

Josie left with my copy of *Seven Habits* and a request to look for behaviors that 'drove her sane.' As long as safety and property damage were not issues with Pete's actions, Josie decided to ignore them.

A few weeks later, Josie told me that our conversation had helped her realize that she had let her thinking make her into a victim. "I wanted to blame Pete's biological mother, my husband, television, video games and Pete's friends for upsetting me. It bothered me when you suggested that I chose to be upset by Pete's behavior. As I read and thought about it, I realized I do have control over my feelings and attitude. Now when I get a little harried, I picture myself in the car driving to "Sanity," population 1."

Josie's eyes crinkled with a smile. "Every day, you have to choose to act instead of react. Being proactive is a habit. A habit I'm glad to work on."

Making Dinner Time Enjoyable

"What's your most difficult time of day?" I asked Sue and Bob, parents of three children under the age of six. They had requested a conference for advice about table manners.

"Dinner time," Sue answered without hesitation. "Definitely dinnertime. It's crazy. The kids are up and down. They don't eat what I've fixed. It's a zoo and I feel like we're not doing anything right."

"Besides eating what do you hope to accomplish at dinner time?" I asked.

Bob gave me a blank look and then grinned. "I hadn't thought about it like that. We're trying to do a lot, aren't we?"

Teaching manners, prayers, thankfulness, trying new foods, fostering family communication and establishing a family ritual of being together were important items for Bob and Sue. No wonder they felt overwhelmed by "table manners."

My next request was "Describe your perfect family dinner."

Sue shook her head. "This is going to sound far-fetched, but it's like we're at an elegant restaurant. Soft lights, candles, classical music in the background, pretty linens and dishes, flowers on the table, interesting conversation. Everyone is smiling and says the food is delicious. And I'm not stuck with cleaning up."

Bob chuckled. "I'm lower maintenance. I'd love to have dinner without raising my voice. If we could have Sue's dream, I'd say that would be perfect."

"Now we have the big picture of what you want. Let's break it into manageable steps and design a six-week action plan," I told them.

Here is Sue and Bob's plan. It's more ambitious than most of us would consider, but I hope you'll see a parenting and planning tool.

Week One: Set the mood with lighting, music, and conversation

Sue and Bob called a family meeting to discuss their desire to change dinnertime. They asked Ben, age five-and-half, Sarah, age four, and two-and-a-half year old Luke, for things they enjoyed and didn't enjoy about dinnertime. The main complaints were not having enough warning to get ready and that it was boring. They decided to dim the lights in the house and play soft music fifteen minutes before dinner was ready. Music and lighting were cues to get washed up and set the table. On Saturday morning when things were not rushed, Sue and Bob showed the children how to set the table. They moved dishes, silverware and placemats so the children could reach them. Sue and Bob planned to tell a story about their day or childhood to make the meal less "boring."

Week Two: Focus on prayer and thankfulness

Sue put a candle that wouldn't tip easily near the table and lit it after everyone was seated. The candle became the signal for prayer and stillness. The answering machine kept the phone from interrupting dinner. Sue or Bob blew out the candle to conclude mealtime, which served as a sign for everyone to thank the cook.

Week Three: Flowers, trying new food, and not complaining

Sue purchased five small vases and silk flowers. At family meeting, they made flower arrangements. The vases became part of each place setting and served as a reminder to try each dish without complaining and to be thankful. Sue included raw vegetables with dip at every dinner per the children's request. After the candle was blown out, the children could fix a peanut butter sandwich if they were still hungry.

Week Four: Learning to clean-up

This week, the children were shown how to carry dishes and put them in the dishwasher, practicing with clean dishes. Bob supervised the dishwasher as the children cleared the table. Sue promised to stay calm if a dish broke.

Week Five: Additional clean-up

Sue and Bob showed the children how to wipe off the table, sweep under the table, and tuck in the chairs. Sue found a child sized broom and dustpan and cut sponges in half to be the right size for small hands to squeeze dry.

Week Six: At last!

Dinnertime was going so well, Bob and Sue wondered why they had been upset about it. "Everything is not perfect," Sue confessed. "We give 'friendly reminders' and re-teach if someone forgets something. The nights that Bob is out of town are harder." Bob added, "The kids are great. They know what we expect and they try hard to do it. It can fall apart, though, if they're tired or sick. We feel so successful that we've started a plan for bath and bedtime."

Even if Sue and Bob's dinner plans are too elaborate for you, I hope you can use this tool to change challenging situations. You'll be able to turn screams into dreams.

To plan change:

- Step back and get the big picture of what's important to you.
- Make an action plan with family input.
- Share the plan with all family members.
- Be clear about expectations.
- Realize that some steps in your plan may take weeks or longer.
- Have fun as you implement your plan and make adjustments when something doesn't work.

Finding the Teachable Moment

Children make us into adults, goes an old saying.

"That's because," Monica added, "they give us our most embarrassing moments."

"For example, at gymnastics class the other day, Danielle, my three-year-old, told the instructor she wasn't going to get off the mat. She smarted off and told her instructor she was going to somersault as long as she wanted and the instructor couldn't stop her. I was shocked at what came out of her mouth. Danielle's tone was so ugly, I was taken off guard. I was, am, embarrassed by her behavior. I feel I'm responsible for it. At home she can be demanding, but I have never seen her act like this. I didn't know what to do or say to make the situation better. I'm embarrassed Danielle could act that way."

The three-year begins to make us "pay for our raising." They can say things that seem to come out of nowhere, putting us in awkward situations. One of my grandfather's favorite stories about me (there were a few!) was about taking me shopping. Driving home, we stopped at an intersection across from a police car. I stuck my head out of the window and yelled to the police officer, "Help! Help! A mean man is kidnapping me!"

My age: almost three years to the day. My granddad knew the officer and from that day forward the officer always knew me. Officer Charlie used the incident as a teachable moment. He let me know that I should scream for help only if I needed it. He told my granddad, "Well, Earl, it sounds like she watched last week's *Highway Patrol*."

As adults, we've learned to tune "out" certain information. Our three, four and five-year-olds are absorbing information from everywhere, trying to connect information with experience. At age three, I must have thought you yelled when you saw a police car since I saw it on television. My mismatch of information and experience led to an embarrassing moment for my grandfather. Almost a heart attack according to him.

We can prepare our children indirectly for certain situations by giving short lessons before and after new experiences. *The teachable moment is rarely the moment when something undesirable is occurring.* In Monica's situation, before gym class she could give Danielle a lesson on "how to say no respectfully," or a lesson on "how to do what your teacher asks." Monica could also tell the gym teacher that she expects Danielle to follow directions and be respectful. If Danielle is disrespectful during class, she could ask the instructor to give Danielle a friendly reminder by saying, "Remember Danielle? I am the teacher and your mom wants you to do this cheerfully."

In some instances, removing a rebellious child may be indicated to avoid disruption of the class.

We also need to make sure we have realistic expectations for behavior. In Danielle's gymnastic class, the instructor may not be considering the learning style of three-year-olds. There may be too much emphasis on following directions instead of exploring movement. We need to make expectations for behavior clear to both our children and the other adults in their lives.

Before entering a new situation with your child, think of the information that is necessary for a successful experience. Beforehand Monica could have watched the gym class to help Danielle prepare for a new situation and visited the instructor to discuss expectations for Danielle's behavior, along with a game plan for dealing with uncooperative behavior.

There will always be embarrassing moments with our children. Being prepared and looking for the teachable moment may lessen the sting. Perhaps we'll also have a humorous incident to tell our grandchildren.

Seek First to Understand and Then to Be Understood

"One is none. Two is ten." — *Icelandic proverb about children*

For a while, this parenting stuff can seem like you've got it under control. Then comes the second child. As Uncle Norm told me years ago, "Before I had children I had ten theories about raising children. Now I have ten children and no theories."

As a new parent a cold lack of confidence in the pit of my stomach seemed to never go away. I appreciated the humorous assurances "my elders" could give me. Now I know that there are guiding principles of human relations that can give us confidence about heading in the right direction and can calm our apprehensions about raising children.

Principles from Stephen Covey's book, *The Seven Habits of Highly Effective People*, are some that I have found to be invaluable. One is "Seek first to understand, and then to be understood."

Part of my training as a Montessori teacher is to observe the child at work. At its essence, observing the child engaged in an activity gives us a window to understand who he or she is.

What an uncommon thing it is in our lives to have someone desire to understand us. Someone who will put their own work, attitudes and prejudices aside to observe us, searching to understand our uniqueness.

As we observe our children at play and at work, or in other words, engaged in purposeful activity, we get an understanding of who they are, their likes and dislikes, their strengths and weaknesses. These observations allow us to be truly helpful to the child, especially a child whom we may view as difficult, unpleasant, or problematic.

As we seek to understand through observation, we will see patterns emerge in a child's behavior. Perhaps a tantrum frequently occurs between 9:30 and 9:45 a.m. Offering a snack at 9:00 a.m. results in no more tantrums.

Perhaps a child who is "naughty" (one who does what he or she ought not) picks all of the neighbor's tulips. Our first impulse might be to make the child understand what he or she did wrong. We could try to be understood first by lecturing on "Don't pick the neighbors flowers." If we seek first to understand, then we might see the incident as an insight to the child's personality.

By seeking first to understand, we might see the child's love of flowers, desire to be helpful by making a flower arrangement, and desire for beauty. Understanding the child first, will help the child understand us.

Later, we can feed the child's interest by giving the names of different flowers, showing how to do flower arrangements, naming the parts of flowers, and drawing flowers. Another issue, of course, is to teach respect for other people's property.

We might approach the child this way, "Dennis, I see you picked Mr. Wilson's tulips. Aren't they beautiful? Oh, you picked them for me? Dennis, that is very thoughtful of you, but these flowers are Mr. Wilson's. He might be sad that they aren't in his yard anymore. We might be sad if our flowers were gone. Let's put them in a vase and take them to Mr. Wilson. We need to tell him we're sorry about picking without permission."

Guiding children is a challenging joy. When we see our job as helping children discover themselves and their purpose, perhaps we can lay aside our need to be understood, and seek to understand children first. This understanding will lead us to be true helpers to our children. In return, children will seek to understand those things we need them to understand, such as, "Please, please, don't pick Mr. Wilson's flowers."

Help Me Help Myself

Children from about age three are asking us to help them learn independence. Children want to learn how to do things on their own without adult supervision or permission. Even though at times we feel we have to help children constantly, in reality, children are asking us to help them help themselves.

Much of what we classify as "misbehavior" in three to six-year-olds, upon closer inspection, is about children trying to do things by themselves, and not being successful. In our hurried world, it's easier to do it ourselves than to stop and show our children how to do a task, and patiently wait as they complete it. Do we really have 15 minutes every morning for our three-year-old to put on her shoes and socks?

Visiting friends a few years ago, I asked their nine-year-old if he'd like to help me cut apples for a pie. Jimmy's eyes widened. "Oh, no, I can't. Mom won't let me use a knife."

"Why is that? Were you irresponsible with a knife?"

"No. Mom's afraid I'll cut myself."

After getting an okay with Jimmy's mom, I began showing him how to cut the apples into chucks after I'd peeled and quartered them. Within half an hour, Jimmy had learned how to peel, quarter and cube apples. And not a mangled finger in sight. At dinner Jimmy was so proud of "our" pies. He thanked me for taking the time to show him how to use a paring knife. "I knew I could do it if someone just let me." Help me help myself.

We can begin to show our children how to use serious tools such as knives, scissors, hammers, and screwdrivers around age three, with 100 percent adult supervision. First, we need to feel confident that the child will listen and follow our direction. If not, he or she is not ready for these kinds of tasks.

Secondly, we need to find tools that are safe. For helping in the kitchen a small butter knife or canapé knife will cut bananas and apple slices, but won't cut small fingers. There are scissors available that will only cut paper, and not hair or clothes. Small hammers can be used to drive 16 penny-nails into log end. For hammering, invest in a pair of child sized safety goggles. A short three-inch screwdriver and ratchet can be used to loosen and tighten screws and bolts on boards.

As a child's level of skill and responsibility grow, we can introduce new levels of difficulty with different tools and materials.

Giving our children "real" work with real tools will help them gain independence. Self-esteem is based on having skills, meaning you can act in ways that benefit yourself and others. Too often, adults think that just telling someone that they are wonderful develops a feeling of self worth. Self-esteem is based on the self-confidence of knowing how to do something, not on what someone says to you.

"Help me help myself" is the young child's cry for independence that leads to true confidence and self-esteem. Don't do for your child what they can do for themselves. Remember, any unnecessary help is an obstacle to a person's independence.

The Prepared Environment

"Pretend that you just found out that you'll have to be in a wheel chair for a year, possibly longer. What adjustments would you have to make to your home to accommodate this change? This week crawl around your house, through every room, and make a list of changes that you would make. That's your homework. See you next week."

Off I went on my hands and knees, antennae up. The things we do as parents. As I crawled, though, I developed some insight into what it might be like to be small and not able to take care of myself.

On the floor, it was not pretty. My kitchen was a dark canyon, with workspace out of reach. Food and dishes were in the upper cabinets. The refrigerator was inaccessible. Unless I tilted my head way back, there was nothing attractive to see.

All my favorite art posters looked distorted from this vantage point.

The dining room was a forest of chair legs. The living room was easier to maneuver, but the couches and chairs were impossible to climb into without standing up. The coffee table and end tables were at a dangerous and eye-poking height.

In the bedroom, I couldn't get into bed by myself. I couldn't open my dresser or the closet doors. In the bathroom, I couldn't climb onto the toilet, reach the sink, or easily get into the bathtub, much less adjust the showerhead. I snagged my pants on the transition piece between the bathroom and hallway.

Negotiating the steps to the garage was treacherous. The trip was rough and dusty, and my hands, along with my clothes, got filthy. The stairs off our wood deck were steep and full of splinters.

Dirty. That was my overall impression of crawling around. With weekly cleaning, I considered my home to be tidy. On my four-legged journey, I discovered grimy lower cabinets, crumbs in the corners, fuzz balls, scribbling under the dining room table (which still surprises me to this day) and splattered windows.

The only objects of interest on this expedition were a bowl and magazines on the coffee table. Pictures and mirrors were hung too high to have any esthetic impact. Doorknobs and light switches were unreachable. The floor was cold and the thermostat might as well been on Mt. Everest. Food and drink were invisible. In my home, I discovered a lowland where I wouldn't want to live. My children were going to spend many years in this land under the table.

Our next parenting session focused on preparing a child friendly environment. Crawling along four months pregnant with our second daughter opened my eyes about creating a special place for our children. A child friendly environment would give my children a home where they could live in dignity and tranquility while learning to manage independently on their own, along with having their own space to work and have meaningful experiences. Experiences beyond finding fuzz balls in the corners.

My husband and I moved the dishes in the kitchen to lower cabinets and found a shelf for snacks. We installed a bottled water dispenser, so our toddler could get her own water easily. We put a small table with chairs in our kitchen and set up a low shelf with puzzles, blocks and other activities.

In the living room we removed the sharp cornered tables and found a Japanese style square coffee table. We added floor pillows, lowered our artwork, put extenders on our light switches and added interesting touchable items to the room, such as baskets of dominoes and wooden blocks, along with some woodcarvings.

In the bathroom we added a plastic step stool that our one-year-old could move to wash her hands, and later brush her teeth and reach the toilet.

In the girls' bedroom, we placed a twin mattress on the floor, and bought a light comforter so Dana could learn to make the bed herself. We removed the closet doors and added lower shelving and rods so the girls could hang up their own clothes and dress themselves.

Of course, we also childproofed cabinets, electrical outlets and moved the "untouchables" to higher cabinets or closets.

These are a few of the efforts we made to prepare a home for our daughters, now in their twenties and in their own homes. To paraphrase a Zen proverb: The journey of a thousand smiles begins with a single crawl.

Removing Obstacles to Development

If we wanted to raft the Grand Canyon, how would we prepare for the trip?

Depending on our experience level, we might arrange for a guide to navigate us down the river. We'd want to learn about the nature and force of the river. We would want to be familiar with dangerous parts of the river. We might practice some drills in case of mishaps, such as what to do if the raft flips. We would want to be as prepared as possible.

In the course of our lives, we will experience a variety of challenges, some as fast and treacherous as rapids, waterfalls, whirlpools, or hydraulics; or as monotonous and slow as pools and eddies.

Isn't life like that? We want it to be challenging enough to be exhilarating, to feel like an adventure. When events happen abruptly, things can become dangerous or overwhelming; too slow and we are bored out of our minds.

What are some of the hazards we'll meet in our children's development? There are two basics kinds of obstacles. One type is external to us. External obstacles act like the water, rocks and boulders in a river. Internal factors, such as personality, knowledge, experience, attitude, character, etc. make up other obstructions.

How do we recognize that a child is facing a challenge? When a child is not developing concentration or independence, we should begin looking for a source, either outside the child's control, or as part of the child's internal make-up. Lack of independence and concentration can take on a variety of forms, much like water in a river. For the child with high energy and strong personality, obstacles may precipitate turbulent and explosive behavior. For the quiet child, the obstacle may thwart the child's progress, as if he or she were caught in a backwater eddy.

External factors. Looking at external sources of obstacles, we need to ask the following:

1. Does the child's environment offer an opportunity to work in peace and dignity to develop him or herself?

2. Does the environment offer a wide social experience?

3. Does the environment offer protection from physical and psychological harm?

4. Does the environment offer adequate challenges for personal growth?

Internal factors. When considering internal factors, ask these questions:

1. Is your child an optimist or a pessimist? An introvert or an extrovert?

Research shows that parental guidance can help a pessimistic or quiet child develop a cheerful or more outgoing life.

2. What developmental stage is your child?

About every three years in the growth of a child, there are profound changes in how and what the child learns. Be aware of these stages.

3. Is the child having a physical response to the environment?

Is the lack of concentration or independence due to allergies, illness, learning or perceptual differences, hearing, vision, diet, sleep, changes in routine, visitors in the house, family member out of town, death in the family, birth of a sibling, arguments in the family, television viewing, or video/computer games?

Observe the child at work and play. Is the child's observable behavior inhibiting independence or concentration?

If yes, examine the external and internal factors of the situation. Decide a plan of action. We can stop the behavior by removing the obstacle, or by taking the child away from the obstacle.

Johnny was failing math, until he started using graph paper to keep the numbers in line. Kayla missed weeks of school due to being allergic to the classroom rabbit. Kevin had given up trying to read because his best friend called him stupid. Mary's grades dropped in a nine-week period while she complained she couldn't see the chalkboard. Steven started a fight every night at bedtime with his father when his dad had been out of town the previous week. Deena threw tantrums about toilet training because she was afraid of falling into the toilet. Obstacles are common, varied, and frequent.

With planning we can avoid many obstacles, and there will be situations we cannot anticipate. Understanding the nature of obstacles, and the nature of the child, may help us "row, row, row our boat, gently down the stream."

Some Alternatives to Saying "No"

There are some days in February that seem as if all we do as parents is say "no."

"No, Susan can't spend the night. Your brother has the flu."

"No, you cannot go bike riding right now. It's dark."

"No, we can't go to the mall. It's supposed to start snowing soon."

Bad weather, illnesses, and long nights seem to conspire to make the shortest month of the year the longest.

Add to this wintry mix, children who, when hearing the word "no," see it as a call to arms, as a personal attack on their independence, and turn all their pent up energy and frustrations toward their parents. These children throw tantrums, scream, call names, stomp off, slam doors, and pout. I hope none of these darlings have been at your house, but if needed, read on.

How can we stand firm when we must answer negatively to a request, while at the same time side-step confrontation, maintain harmony in the household, and allow our children to preserve their independence and dignity? Did I include, "retain our sanity"?

Here are some helpful hints from the book, *How to Talk So Kids Will Listen, and Listen So Kids Will Talk.* First published in 1980, this book was one of the first on my parenting shelves, and I wouldn't doubt that I purchased it in February.

Give information. When met with a situation, we can give information that will help the child figure out that right now is not a good time.

For, "Mom, can I invite Jimmy over to play?" instead of saying, "No, you can't," give decision making facts.

"Dinner will be ready in ten minutes."

You don't have to say no, and your child should have enough information to see that the answer is in fact "no."

Accept feelings. Sometimes we can lessen our children's disappointment or frustration if they sense we understand their feelings.

"But Dad, I don't want to go to bed right now."

Instead of no, we might say, "I can understand if it were up to you, you would stay up all night so you wouldn't miss a thing."

Describe the problem. "Mom, can Lucy spend the night?"

"I'd like to say yes, but your grandparents are coming this weekend."

Give yourself time to think. Your child says, "Dad, can I have a horse at my birthday party?"

You can respond, "Let me think about it, please."

When possible, substitute a 'yes' for a 'no.' Your child asks, "Can we go to the mall?"

Instead of saying, "No, I've got to finish the laundry," you could say, "Yes, just as soon as the laundry is folded and put away."

These suggestions may seem like a lot of work and the hard way to say no. But considering some of the drama we may encounter, sometimes the high road is the short cut to where we want to go.

If none of these works for you, there is always, "Because I said so." We can move, next, to other languages: Nein. Nichts. Non. Nej. Nyet.

Lead or Manage?

As parents we lead and manage our children. If we lead without adequate management skills, logistical problems arise. If we manage without providing clear leadership, we may travel a long road to nowhere.

Leadership focuses on developing people, empowerment, doing the right things, direction and principles. Management, on the other hand, concerns itself with taking care of things, control, doing things right, speed and practices.

If we are leading in the wrong direction, does it matter how well managed the journey is? Conversely, when our leadership can't manage to do things right, control outcomes and practices with a modicum of speed and sense of delivery, is our leadership effective?

Leading is an art. Managing is more about skills and organization. Parenting is the delicate balance of knowing when to guide and when to supervise.

Paul was a time management guru and didn't go anywhere or do anything without consulting his Daily Planner. For Paul, it came naturally to schedule time everyday to develop new skills. Fitness training was inked in from 5 to 6 am everyday while Paul listened to tapes to learn French. Dinner was from 6 to 6:30 pm. After dinner, every 15 minutes in the Daily Planner included activities for Paul to oversee with his children. Piano practice, read books, yoga exercises, bath time, tooth brushing, and prayers. Paul scheduled every minute of his day. Paul planned his wife's activities. Paul's children's events were in the book. By golly, Paul said, in his family they got things done. The Daily Planner organized everything.

As Paul's children began to enter into the independent stage of the older child, around age six years, small actions of rebellion and deception began to appear in the children's behavior. Dawdling at the dinner table in order to miss piano practice. Going to get a drink of water in the kitchen when it was time to brush teeth. Hiding the reading books. The children's passive acts of rebellion sabotaged Paul's Daily Planner.

Paul made the mistake of managing his children when they needed his leadership for vision, moral direction, and personal development. For Paul the balance of leadership and management tipped completely towards taking care of the schedule, controlling time and practices, and being efficient.

When we become overly concerned with controlling things and people, instead of empowering others to manage and control themselves, we may find ourselves surrounded by indications of low trust. Some of these symptoms, but by no means all, are escapism, anger, fear, chaos, in-fighting, back-biting, hidden agendas, withholding of information, poor-me attitudes, and people saying one thing and doing another.

To effectively manage we must lead. To lead we must effectively manage. So the dance begins.

Our job as parents and teachers is to have a clear direction on how we are going to help our children learn to lead and manage themselves, so that later they may in turn, lead and manage others.

Otherwise, we may end up in a place we never intended, using a map to obscurity, but running right on time.

Paying Attention to the Right Stuff

In my elementary and junior high school years I always sat in the back row. Except in my seventh grade English class.

I wondered why I inevitably sat in the back against the wall. Alphabetic order I presumed. The back row perspective allowed me to observe everyone in my classrooms, and even as a second grader I could see that the children on the front two rows got most, if not all, of the teacher's smiles and pats on the back.

The concrete block walls chilled and isolated. Not until I was in my thirties and reading a book on classroom management did I understand why I sat at the back of the classroom.

There is a strategy of assigning students to the front of the room who need help to stay on task. Children who follow direction and work independently are put in the back of the room. In retrospect, occupying the rear seat was sort of a backhanded compliment.

Troublemakers, though, never sat on the back row. From the cold wall the troublemakers looked like the teacher's pets.

On the back row, we were marooned in a sea of desks a thousand miles away from a smile.

The front row strategy, I admit, was effective. Our classrooms ran smoothly as teachers paid attention to those children who needed firm and vigilant direction to learn, and encouraged them with a word, a smile, or a touch of the hand on the back.

My teachers taught their inattentive students to pay attention to the right stuff. My teachers knew that to help children learn to do the right things, you have to catch children doing something right, instead of catching them doing something wrong.

When we give undue attention to behavior that doesn't benefit the child's efforts in building concentration and independence, we inadvertently create a reason for the child to continue the "wrong" behavior in order to get attention.

Ignoring unacceptable behavior can be difficult, but we should only stop the behavior if it is dangerous to people or property. We need to catch our children doing something right and let them know unequivocally that they are on the path to independence and stronger focus. How else are they to understand when they are headed in a positive direction?

Three-year-old Bobby, the youngest of four children, pulled stunts to get attention by jumping on the dinner table, throwing his dishes, or running out the front door. Bobby was an expert at provoking a sibling's tirade or inducing a round of laughter. Unless Bobby did something outrageous his family was too busy to notice him.

Bobby's behavior stemmed from a need to belong. Bobby's antics met with such success that that he created more outrageous behavior daily. Not knowing what else to do, Bobby's parents and siblings decided to take their pediatrician's advice and catch Bobby doing something right.

"The first day," Bobby's mother, Kay said, "the only thing positive I could find was that Bobby got in his booster seat by himself. But we resolved to not give Bobby any attention for his disruptive behaviors, and made a concentrated effort to pay attention to him before he demanded our attention with some stunt."

"In a couple of weeks, as we focused on Bobby and gave him attention for those positive behaviors, Bobby's mischievous stunts became less frequent. In a month they were gone."

Let's pay attention to the right stuff, even for the kids on the back row.

Balancing Parenthood

Every now and then go away,
Have a little relaxation,
For when you come back to your work
Your judgment will be surer;
Since to remain constantly at work
Will cause you to lose power of judgment.
Go some distance away
Because the work appears smaller
And more of it
Can be taken in at a glance,
And a lack of harmony
Or proportion
Is more readily seen.
  — Leonardo Da Vinci (1452-1519)

"Heather is five-years-old and I've never left her. Not a night away. Not a babysitter," Betsey said as though it were a badge of honor.

The joy we experience as new parents bonds us to our children. We want to be close. To provide food and protection, we must be nearby. Babies and young children require holding and hugging to feel loved. To meet these childhood needs, parents have two basic tasks. We have to invest time with our children, and we have to be able to see each child's point of view.

From the moment of conception, parents balance personal needs and desires with the needs of their unborn child. We eat right. We avoid unhealthy substances. We try to think pleasant thoughts. We listen to whale songs. We get extra sleep. We buy hundreds of dollars of baby supplies.

Caring for a newborn takes 110% of our time. A newborn depends totally on his or her mother and father. The mother depends on the father for strength and encouragement. These new relationships consume us, as well they should.

Parenting is an intense and satisfying activity with a "gotchya." The gotchya? Parents are to produce an independent adult from a helpless seven-pound being. We have to go from caring for an infant who needs us 24 hours a day, to being the parent of adult who doesn't need us at all.

Parents tell us they want their adult children to possess these qualities:

Happiness, confidence, independence, responsibility, respectfulness, a loving and giving nature, excitement about life, self-motivation, life-long-learning, financial security, empathy, compassion, integrity, and to be a world-citizen.

These attributes are the long-term goals we have for our children, and not surprisingly, for ourselves.

Our children can achieve these qualities, if we consider two questions:

1. What do our children need and how can we meet their needs?

2. Are we focused more on our children's behavior than their needs?

Focusing on our children's needs to help achieve our long-term goals means that we have to relinquish control of the process. We have to focus on needs instead of behavior. Because in the end, the process of child rearing is not about what we want. It's about what our children need to become fully functioning adults.

Betsy's comment about never spending a night away from her daughter made me wonder whose needs were being served, mother or daughter's. It is important to know that "every now and then" we need to step away from our work to get a perspective and to see if all is in proportion. As a friend of mine says, "Take a reality check."

Let's heed Da Vinci's advice to "have a little relaxation" and make the time to step back from our work with our children. It should help us get a view of the big picture, and "enhance our power of judgment" to see what our children need in their journey to adulthood.

Parents are the Real Thing

"Humans would degenerate without the child to help him rise. If the adult does not waken little by little, a hard crust will form around him and make him insensible." —Dr. Maria Montessori

Being in the city is interesting, to say the least. Surrounded by world-class restaurants with scores of ethnicities, shops, theatres, museums, galleries, and on and on, the choices for activities are immense.

It's a beautiful fall afternoon. I sit on a park bench people watching, and I think that in the city we extend childhood. I see adults but few children. In the city, we adults amuse ourselves with our latte, our sushi, our lectures, our happy hours, and our 24-hour gym memberships. But I sense, where there are seldom children, there are not many true adults.

There are dogs in the park, chasing balls, and wagging their tails. Domestic dogs retain the puppy gesture of a tail wag, because emotionally and socially pet dogs do not mature into adults. These playful animals are mature biological specimens, but they are not the adults of their species.

Two athletic tan guys drive up in their German made convertible, the kind with three letters in the name, not two. They toss a Frisbee and talk about the party they went to last night and the one for tonight.

Across the street, two thirty-ish women, come out of the salon, high-heeled, manicured, pedicured, and outfitted for an evening at the new trendy spot.

I grin, remembering how in my early twenties, the pursuit of being hip, dressing right, eating out, allured me. Not much of that, though, helped me become a better person.

Then came parenthood. What a wake-up call for character development. Being responsible for small human beings, day in and day out, year after year, created qualities in my personality that I never imagined.

From the beginning, our children reflect our best and worst traits, if we can bear to look in this mirror. These reflections help make us into a better person by showing us our strengths and uncovering our weaknesses. Our relationships with our children force us to decide what kind of person we want to become.

So in those moments of parenthood when we dream of a bit more "adult" sophistication with images of carrying an evening bag instead of a diaper bag, or wish we were pushing seventy in a sports car instead of pushing a stroller, remember this: that the job you are doing as a parent is the most important job on this earth. That as a parent you are your child's first and best teacher and ally. That you are stronger than you realize.

Remember, in your low moments, that real people are walking around with babies, instead of the newest electronic music maker. Real people are taking kids on a walk instead of taking golf lessons. Real people are reading "Goodnight Moon" for the thousandth time instead of the latest novel.

To you, dear parents of all ages, I say thank you. Thank you for being the adult. Thank you for having the courage, the sense of adventure, and the sense of humor to continue the human race.

GARGOYLES
Dealing with External Forces

---

he roof of a building protects us from the forces of wind and weather. The roof of a cathedral had to be hoisted up piece by piece 16 stories and higher. Once in place the roof protected the cathedral interior from rain, snow, heat and other elements.

We also have to build protection around our families from external forces that diminish, deteriorate and destroy the fortress of our family. Even with the best foundations and supporting structures there are natural forces we have to face that can be unpleasant.

It requires considerable effort to hoist the coverings to protect our foundation of love, family and work, and to shield the character strengths that rest on that foundation.

Unchecked water flow creates structural problems for a building. The gargoyles on the roof of the cathedral were designed to be down spouts, diverting the water away from the roof and foundation of the building.

Gargoyles resemble phantasmagorical beings and range from looking like demons and grotesque monsters to humorous renditions of people and animals.

Working with our children we have to deal with unpleasant events and behaviors—our children, and perhaps ourselves, appearing at times like spouting gargling gargoyles.

Our children's behaviors and emotions are natural indicators of obstacles to development and unmet needs. Gargoyles can remind us to look for these obstacles and needs.

The spouting of the gargoyles is a normal response to the natural event of rain. If we have prepared ourselves with an adequate roof, foundation, and structural support, as well as being aware of the effects of external forces, we should see our "gargoyles" for what they are—devices that divert from our foundations the natural but sometimes destructive forces of unmet needs and developmental obstacles.

How to Know When Development Is Going Awry

"Is my child going through a stage or is something wrong?" is a question that runs though our minds, usually in the wee hours of the morning. We worry because the question addresses the art of being a parent, that is, knowing when to act and when to step back and watch.

For the young child, learning skills and appropriate behavior doesn't follow a straight line. Instead it is a zigzag path of peaks and valleys. As parents we can be mystified when Wednesday night Sarah can get her pajamas on all by herself, and on Thursday she can't and cries in frustration.

It requires a lot of patience, (I'm talking mythical and biblical here), for us as parents and teachers to deal with these ups and downs. It is important for us to follow through when giving instructions. For example, if you've asked your four-year-old to set the table for dinner, you need to be prepared to re-teach the skill, or walk through the job with your child, and then remind them to do it each night, until he or she can be fully responsible. While learning to set the table, children have many details to remember, such as how many places to set, where to place the plates and utensils, filling water glasses, etc. We need to be there to assure success.

Learning skills and memorizing rules of behavior can take frequent repetition for child and parent. One familiar lament we might remember from our childhoods is "How many times do I have to tell you to close the door?" We need to understand the answer may be a "few gad zillion."

Certain skills may take a long time to develop. If you are concerned that your child is not developing an age appropriate skill, write down in your calendar one month ahead the desired skill, such as "close the door properly." When you see on the calendar after a month of re-teaching that the skill has not progressed, visit with your pediatrician about your concerns.

Behavior is of course a key component to our children's development. In normal development we should observe children that are joyful, pleasant, eager to please and connected to their families and homes. Two "emotional vitamins" for proper child development, recommended by Robert Shaw, M.D., are clear structure and expectations.

Dr. Robert Shaw, author of *The Epidemic: The Rot of American Culture, Absentee and Permissive Parenting, and the Resultant Plague of Joyless, Selfish Children*, says that "excessive tantrums, persistent bedtime issues and aggression towards playmates" are signs that development is going awry in the three to six-year-old. These behaviors are a cry from the child for the parent to take charge and provide clear family structure and expectations for behavior. If unacceptable behaviors are given in to and the child placated, you have started on the path to a defiant unruly child. Left unchallenged, the child's behavior will become more and more difficult to handle.

As parents and teachers we need to observe our children's behavior. If a behavior, such as not closing a door properly, is due to weak skills, we need to teach and re-teach the skill, then wait and watch. If the behavior is defiant, rude, unkind or aggressive, we need to act immediately to stop it. We can eliminate tantrums, along with defiant, aggressive and unkind behaviors, by providing clear structure and expectations.

When you are lying awake at night, concerned about your child's behavior, ask yourself these two questions:

1. Is my child's behavior due to needing to learn a skill?

2. Is my child's behavior due to a lack of clear expectations for behavior and clear family structure?

With the answers to these two questions, you'll know what you need to do.

Dealing with Tantrums

The day that your child turns red then blue while writhing on the floor in an attempt to get his or her way, is a day when you earn perhaps your first parenting medal, "valor under stress."

Joan, a mother of two, related to me her ordeal of a temper tantrum with three-year-old Robbie.

"It started with such a silly thing. We had told Robbie he couldn't go with his dad to the store after lunch. Robbie spent the next forty-five minutes screaming and crying. Bob finally had enough and said Robbie could go. Bob felt guilty that Robbie had spent all this time upset, when it was supposed to be "quality" Dad time. But I think Bob shouldn't have given in to Robbie's tantrum."

"I can see how Bob was feeling," I said. "But Bob violated the Tommy Lee Jones rule."

"What rule is that?"

"It's from a movie, *US Marshals*, where Tommy Lee Jones' character states, 'I don't negotiate with terrorists.' It works with children, too."

"If Robbie takes you 'hostage' with a tantrum, you can't give in to his demands. If you do, Robbie will learn that a tantrum works and next time he'll be prepared to go a little longer to get his way. A forty-five minute tantrums tells me that this is not the first one."

"You're right," Joan blushed. "Robbie's so different than our easy-going six-year-old. How can we help Robbie?"

Tantrums usually begin before a child is fully verbal. We, as parents, in all fairness, try to meet our children's needs. Inadvertently we allow tantrums to grow by reinforcing the child's belief that a tantrum is an effective communication tool. When we give in to a tantrum, the child has found a powerful way to get what he wants.

"It's not going to be pleasant to help Robbie stop his tantrums. First you must remember the Tommy Lee Jones Rule and be prepared to ride it out. You must be firm, yet kind."

"Talk with Robbie and tell him something like this: "My job is to help you learn how to be a happy. When you scream and cry I know I have to help you. When you get upset, I'll ask you to use your words to tell me how you feel. If you can't do that I'll ask you to go to your room until you can talk to me. If you don't go to your room I'll walk you in. Do you understand? I love you and want you to learn to be happy."

"If Robbie starts to throw a tantrum, kindly remind him about your talk. Remind him to use his words. If Robbie can't calm down, ask him to go to his room until he can talk to you. If he refuses, carry him in and kindly tell him that he may leave when he feels like talking. Say something like—I love you but you need to learn how deal with your tantrums."

"Sometimes, a child will learn that tantrums aren't going to work anymore on the first test of the rule. For others it takes a few times. Remember, don't be held hostage."

Joan and Bob were successful at communicating to Robbie about their expectations for his behavior, and didn't negotiate. Robbie's tantrums ended.

If tantrums continue, keep a written record of when and why they occur. A pattern should appear according to time, place and situation. Tiredness, hunger, a parent being gone, or over stimulation may be trigger factors that will become evident.

Tantrums can become a learned behavior to control others. Unfortunately, we all know adults who use tantrums to get their way. As a friend of mine says, "It's not pretty." Perhaps imagining our child in a tantrum at age thirty may help us have that right amount of firmness, kindness and courage.

Helping Children Deal With Their Feelings

"I was a wonderful parent before I had children. I was an expert on why everyone else was having problems with theirs. Then I had three of my own."

So begins the book, *How To Talk So Kids Will Listen and Listen So Kids Will Talk*. Adele Faber and Elaine Mazlish use humor with their parenting and professional experiences to help parents learn effective communication.

Helping children deal with their feelings is fundamental in creating a parent/child relationship built on respect. Respect, from the Latin *re+spectare*, means to look again or to give a second look. When we have mutual respect, we look each other in the eye again, and again and again. Respect begins with a look.

Faber and Mazlish, both students of Dr. Haim Ginott, tell us that there is a direct connection to how kids feel and how they behave. If kids feel right, they'll act right. We can help them feel right by accepting and respecting their feelings.

It can be easy to dismiss our children's feelings. Children can be over dramatic or use the wrong word to describe their emotions. Taken off guard, we respond with phrases such as— —You're not hungry. You just ate. Or —You're not hot. The air conditioner is running. How about—Don't say you hate your sister. That's an awful thing to say.

Kids can become confused and angry when adults deny children's feelings. Hearing their feelings dismissed teaches our children not to trust their feelings and keeps them from learning to express them appropriately.

Faber and Mazlish recommend four steps in accepting and respecting our children's feelings:

1. We can listen quietly and attentively.

Turn off the television, radio, cell phone, and computer, and give your child your full attention. Listen and refrain from giving advice, judging, asking questions, pitying, psychoanalyzing, or taking sides. Just listen.

2. We can acknowledge our children's feelings with just a word.

Using just a word or two, for example—oh, mmmm, I see——will help our children feel that we are hearing what they are saying and feeling. I've found nodding with steady eye contact acts as an understanding word.

3. We can give the feeling a name.

That sounds frustrating. You must be upset (angry, sad). You must feel happy about that.

4. We can give the child his wishes in fantasy.

"I wish you could wear your pajamas to school."

A three-year-old friend of mine was upset and in tears about having to take turns on our tree swing. I listened for a while then looked Andie in the eye and said, "I think you'd like to swing all day."

Andie nodded through her hiccups.

"It's frustrating to have to take turns with your brothers." Another nod.

"I wish I could build another swing, just for you, so you could swing and swing and swing. I'd write your name on it with pink and silver letters."

Andie wiped her face and gave me a smile. She jumped from her mother's lap and ran to get a ball. Feelings acknowledged. Crisis over. Move on.

When we use these four steps, we'll help our children deal with their emotions. We can accept all feelings. Actions intended to harm are what we should not accept or condone. A child might be angry and express hatred or a desire to harm. We could respond with, "I understand you're upset with your brother. Use your words to tell him what you want. Remember, no hitting."

Listen so kids will talk. Talk so kids will listen. It's a two-way street, built on respect. Look 'em in the eyes and listen, really listen.

Is Your Child Getting Enough Sleep?

Five-year-old Ricky had difficulty focusing in his morning school session and fell asleep during the afternoon work time. After lunch Ricky would start to act 'hyper' and push and hit other children on the playground. When Ricky laid down to rest, he'd be asleep in five minutes and have to be woken for three o'clock dismissal. Leaving school, Ricky would cry because he hadn't gotten to be with his friends.

At our October conference I visited with his mother and father about Ricky's naps. "I guess he just needs more sleep right now. I'm sure Ricky will grow out of his naps soon enough," his father told me.

I regretted not finding out more about Ricky's nighttime schedule at our conference. To most people a five-year-old taking a two or three-hour nap in the afternoon might not seem like a problem. Ricky was bright and energetic and was becoming more frustrated as his friends did classroom and outdoor activities without him. His classmates were learning to read and Ricky felt left out of his work groups.

After a few more weeks of this napping routine, I called Ricky's mother. "What time does Ricky go to bed and get up in the morning," I asked.

"Ricky gets up at six with us and he's in bed by ten," Ricky's mom told me.

As we continued our conversation, I discovered that Ricky had a television, video player, computer and video games in his bedroom. Most nights, Ricky went to sleep with a movie playing in his room. Ricky had expressed his frustration to his parents of feeling left out and not getting along with the other children. I suggested that we work together to try to adjust Ricky's sleeping schedule so that he would be alert, cheerful and productive at school.

Five-year-olds need between 10 to 13 hours of sleep per day. Ricky was getting between 10 and 11 hours of sleep in a routine that worked for him and his parents. To maximize his time with his parents, Ricky went to bed and got up according to his parent's schedule. If Ricky hadn't expressed a desire to work in the afternoon class, or had been more alert during the morning, I might have recommended that he continue to nap. Ricky wasn't happy, and his parents and I agreed to make some changes to help him.

After conferencing with his mother and father, we decided to work on changing his bedtime and wake-up times. We coordinated a weekly schedule where Ricky took half an hour less nap at school and during weekends, and went to bed half an hour earlier. Each week we added another half hour, so that in a month Ricky was in bed by eight every night, and not napping at school. Ricky's father also removed all the electronic equipment from Ricky's bedroom so there would be no distractions for a good night's rest.

In a few weeks Ricky was involved in all the classroom activities and was able to control his actions on the playground. Ricky began to read and "catch-up" with his peers. He was excited about school again, and it was wonderful to see his bright eyes and smile every afternoon.

For more information about your child's sleep requirements, and tips for parents and teachers on solving sleep problems, go to www.sleepforkids.org. Sweet Dreams.

Avoid Discouragement, Apologize

"My dad never apologized for anything. He never admitted he was wrong, made a mistake or said he was sorry. I think that caused so much friction and anger in our relationship. Now, I find I'm starting to do the same thing with my boys," Stewart said during a parenting class. "How can I change?"

We had been talking that evening about ways that parents discourage their children, and that a misbehaving child is always a discouraged child. Stewart recognized himself in our discussion of the four key ways that parents discourage children with negative expectations, focusing on mistakes, perfectionism and overprotection.

Stewart saw his father's inability to apologize as a result of a desire to be seen as perfect. Stewart was realizing that his desire for perfection might create the same kind of discouragement in his children that he had experienced as a child. Stewart wanted a long-term healthy relationship with his boys, then ages three and four.

I shared with Stewart and the group one of my experiences with perfectionism and the power of apologizing. My book club was scheduled to arrive at our home in less than thirty minutes. My daughters were three and four and were helping me prepare snacks and set out plates and napkins. I was a little out of sorts, because my husband was out of town and wasn't home to help put the girls to bed. As we left the kitchen, a glass platter got bumped. Vegetables and dip flew off the counter. Broccoli, celery, and carrot sticks flew across the floor along with shards of glass. Garlic leek dip landed in my shoes.

It was an unfortunate and poorly timed accident. It was not intentional, but I reacted as if it had been masterfully planned. "Upstairs. Now. Both of you. I can't believe you did this. You've ruined everything," I yelled, instantly regretting my lack of self-control. There was no excuse for blowing up even if there was onion dip in my shoes. No excuse.

The girls ran upstairs, upset and crying. I cleaned up the mess, rueful of how I had over reacted. I walked up the stairs and sat down on their bed.

"I'm sorry I lost my temper. I know this was an accident and you didn't mean to knock the plate from the table. I shouldn't have yelled at you. I think I was more concerned about things being perfect for my meeting than your feelings. Will you forgive me? How can I make you feel better?" I choked back my tears.

My daughters patted me on the arm. "It's okay, Mom. We still love you."

Children have such kind, resilient and forgiving natures. We were all children once, and it helps us be better parents when we can remember that.

Don't be afraid of looking out of control or weak to your children when you've done something you wish you hadn't. Say you're sorry, ask for forgiveness and try to make things right. Apologize, and you'll side step those four key ways parents discourage their children. Just apologize.

Be Friendly with Error

Nicholas, a cheerful three-year-old, had cried every day at snack time for a week. Because he had spilt a pitcher of water on the snack table, Nicholas refused to try to pour himself a drink of water. Efforts to encourage Nicholas to pour an eight-ounce pitcher were met with tears. "I can't. I'll spill and make a mess and everybody will be mad at me."

Pouring water in a Montessori classroom is a critical skill because so many other lessons involve water or pouring, such as hand washing, table washing, and cloth washing, to name a few. Nicholas had such a fear of failure, that I didn't know how to get him over this obstacle.

In the middle of the night, when most inspiration seems to arrive, I had an idea. The next morning, I told my classroom assistant that I was going to give a cloth-washing lesson and in the process "accidentally" spill a large pitcher of water. Could she encourage children to set up away from my presentation area to avoid more chaos than necessary?

During the lesson to an older student, I "tripped" and a half-gallon of water rushed over the hardwood floors. "Oops," I laughed, surveying the water. "It's okay. It will clean it up. It's just water."

To my surprise, Nicholas arrived, mop in hand, asking if he could help me.

"That would be lovely," I replied.

Nicholas and I mopped and dried the floor, checking that every drop was gone so our friends wouldn't slip on a wet floor. We laughed and sang, "...down came the rain and washed the spider out. Out came Nicholas to dry up all the rain..."

"When a big person spills, it's a big spill," I joked with Nicholas.

Mike, a four-year-old walked up and said, "See, Nicholas, I told you it's okay to make a mistake at school."

Nicholas broke into a wide grin and turned to put the mop away.

Later that morning, Nicholas came to me. "Ms. Maren, did you spill that water just for me?"

"What do you mean, Nicholas?"

"Did you spill it to make me feel better?"

Now it was my turn to feel as though a bucket of water had just dumped over my head, like in the old 70's Laugh-In Show. Sock-it-to-me. I thought I was a better actress that that. I imagined myself to be more convincing to a three-year-old.

"Thank you, Ms. Maren. I'm not scared to pour anymore." Nicholas gave me a hug.

"You're welcome, Nicholas." I took a deep breath.

Thank you, Nicholas, I thought, for helping me remember to be friendly with error.

Don't Be a Dolt

"I can't tell you 'cause you're a dolt," Kenny said through his sniffles.

"A dolt?" I thought. What did I do to be called a dolt by a kindergartner in my Sunday school class? I ventured into unknown territory.

"Kenny, what do you mean, a dolt?"

"You know, a grown-up."

"Oh, I see. An adult." That was a relief.

"Mike said if I told a dolt, it would be tattling and then he'd really pinch me."

Our Sunday school group was walking back from the Children's Sermon portion of the service when Kenny had burst into tears. Kenny and I were talking in the hallway while my co-teacher took rest of the group into our classroom for snack.

I was down on my knees, eye level with Kenny. This looked like an "active listening" moment.

Active listening is a set of skills that allows adults to help a child handle the child's own problems. Active listening is for situations in which the child owns the problem, or in which the child and the adult share responsibility.

The following five skills are involved in active listening:

1. Listen actively. Be all ears, and restate what you understand.

2. Listen for content.

3. Connect feeling to content.

4. Look for alternatives and/or predict consequences.

5. Follow up.

"So you're upset and hurt because Mike pinched you?" I asked.

"He pinches me every Sunday in church. Mike says, 'Bet I can make you squirm.'" Kenny's upper lip quivered.

"Mike is pinching you in church trying to get you to misbehave."

"He's supposed to be my friend," Kenny hiccupped.

"It feels bad when a friend tries to get you to do the wrong thing."

Kenny nodded. "Please don't tell Mike. He said if I tattled he wouldn't be my friend."

"Would you like me to make sure that Mike doesn't sit next to you during the children's sermon?" I asked.

"But he's my friend."

"Is there something else we can try so he won't bother you?"

Kenny looked straight at me. "I think I need to tell him to stop. That it's not okay to pinch me."

"Would you like me to be there when you tell Mike?"

"No, but I think I'll tell my mom." Kenny wiped his eyes with the back of his hand.

"Kenny, let me know how it goes when you tell Mike that it's not okay to pinch you."

"Okay. I'm ready for cookies." Kenny turned and walked into the room.

Since Kenny and I shared responsibility for his situation, I listened and kept his confidence from Mike. From my end, as an adult, I took the responsibility to make sure that Kenny felt safe. I visited with Kenny and Mike's mothers about the situation. I mailed Mike a note telling him that friends used their hands to help other people, and mentioned ways I had seen him help.

Active listening helps keep communication open and can assist us from reacting with some of the following responses:

1. Commanding. "Stop the crying, Kenny."
2. Give advice. "Just don't sit by Mike."
3. Placate or distract. "Go have a cookie, two cookies."
4. Moralize. "I'll tell Mike that is wrong."
5. Use sarcasm. "Aren't you a crybaby."
6. Act like a know it all. "Just tell Mike to stop it."
7. Play psychologist. "Mike's having some problems right now."

These kinds of responses can block communication and not help the child learn to solve the problem independently.

Don't be a dolt. Practice active listening.

Alternatives to Punishment

Six-year old Bobby walks into the kitchen from playing soccer. Bobby's dad, Tom, had asked Bobby to take off his muddy shoes before entering the house. Red Georgia mud dotted the new hallway and den carpet.

When Tom sees the footprints, he is furious about the mess and that Bobby had disobeyed him. "Bobby," Tom says, his voice rising, "for disobeying me, you'll not be able to watch TV for a week. And John won't be able to come and spend the night on Friday."

Bobby starts to cry and runs up the stairs yelling, "You're the meanest dad in the world. I hate you."

Punishment for misbehavior can have the undesirable consequences of resentment and anger that can damage our parent/child relationship, perhaps forever. What alternatives to punishment do we have?

In their book, *How to Talk so Kids Will Listen*, Faber and Mazlish give seven alternatives to punishment in order to help children learn and exhibit appropriate behavior.

1. Point out a way to be helpful. Tom could have phrased his command differently. "Bobby, it would be helpful if you would take off your shoes on the porch and clean them outside." Or after the dastardly deed was done, "It would be helpful if you would sit down right now and take off those shoes. Then you can help me clean up the mud stains."

2. Express strong disappointment of the action without attacking the person's character.

Tom could have said, "Bobby, I'm disappointed that the carpet is muddy from your soccer shoes. I asked you to take your shoes off before coming into the house."

3. State your expectations. "Bobby, I expect you to listen to me and do what I ask."

4. Show child how to make amends.

"Bobby, after you take your shoes off, you'll need to help me clean the carpet. If the mud doesn't come out, I want you to go with me to rent a carpet cleaner."

5. Give a choice.

"Bobby, if you want to continue playing soccer, you need to remember to take your shoes off before you come into the house. You need to pay attention when I tell you to do something. Forget to take off your shoes, then no soccer. You decide."

6. Take action.

If Tom's given a choice, such as the choice given above, Tom will have to take action if Bobby forgets to take off his shoes again.

7. Allow the child to experience the consequences of his misbehavior.

"Bobby, since I'll have to clean the carpet tomorrow, I won't be able to take you to the movies like we had planned.'

If our goal is to help our children learn appropriate behavior, punishment may not be an effective way for the child to see his mistake.

When dealing with misbehavior, try using one of these seven alternatives to avoid anger, resentment and discouragement in your child and to help build a trusting loving parent/child relationship.

It may take a lot of practice to catch our reactions, but I think you'll find it's worth it.

Punishing with Rewards

A fishbowl full of candy sat on the third grade teacher's desk.

"When you've finished your math assignment you can choose a piece of candy," Ms. Marsh said as she handed out worksheets.

All but two of the students went to work. Tamika and Jennifer looked out the window, math sheets untouched. Tamika began her calculations as the first students turned in papers. Jennifer never picked up her pencil.

At lunch, I sat down and visited with the girls about what I had observed.

"Jennifer," I said, "why didn't you work on your math assignment?"

"Well," Jennifer said, "I don't like math and I don't like that kind of candy, so why bother?"

Tamika joined in. "I like math, but I don't like being treated like a baby." Her voice changed to a high-pitched singsong. "Here baby, baby. Do your mathy-wathy and you can have some candy. Okay, baby?"

Jennifer said, "Yeah, that's kind of how it feels to me."

Tamika continued. "So I challenge myself. I wait until the first person turns in work, then I see if I can get it done, 100 percent correct, by the time the fifth person gets to Ms. Marsh's desk. And I don't like that candy either."

Alfie Kohn in his book, *Punished by Rewards: The Trouble with Gold Stars, Incentive Plans, A's, Praise and other Bribes*, documents how rewarding behavior can create the same kind of discouragement, anger and resentment that is created when punishing behavior. Incentives rarely motivate, and as in the case of Jennifer and Tamika, actually become disincentives.

Kohn recommends that instead of "doing to" our children to change their behavior, we should instead concentrate on "working with" our children to help them understand their personal or intrinsic motivations.

Kohn suggests we can create in our homes and classrooms conditions for authentic motivation by doing four things: Watch, listen, talk and think.

Watch. Watching means we don't keep our children under constant surveillance. We look for problems that need to be solved and help our children solve them. Tamika's parents had taught her how to make a game out of something that she might not otherwise be motivated to do.

Listen. We listen to our children and take their point of view seriously and respectfully. We try to imagine how the situation looks from their point of view. Ms. Marsh, in her desire to motivate her students, had neglected to listen for her students' point of view.

Talk. Talking actually means for us as adults to talk less and ask more questions. We need to encourage our children to talk to us so that we will know what we are doing right, where we need to improve, and how we might change. As a visiting classroom observer, I was able to ask Tamika and Jennifer about their math, and get important feedback.

Think. We need to think about the long-term effects of our strategies when we offer extrinsic rewards. We also need to think about where our strategies come from. Are our strategies based on a preference of using power in our relationships, or a reaction to being controlled by others?

In Ms. Marsh's situation, she had learned about the candy reward system in an in-service presentation. Her school was trying to improve scores on their state mandated math test. Test scores, which did not improve with candied motivation.

If we are committed to helping our children be able and willing to do their best, we need to watch, listen, talk and think to be sure our strategies are building intrinsic motivation and not punishing by rewards.

The Difference Between Discipline and Punishment

"Train up a child in the way he should go and when he is old, he will not depart from it."—Proverbs 22:6

"What is the difference between disciplining a child and punishing a child?" Jeff, father to a two-year-old, wrote in his e-mail. "I don't see any difference. Isn't it the same thing?"

There is a difference, as I explained to Jeff. My e-mail follows:

Jeff, let's look at the definition of these two words from the American Heritage Dictionary.

Punishment: to subject someone to a penalty for a crime, fault or misbehavior. From the Latin *poenire* and the Greek *poine; poena* is money paid as a fine.

Discipline: training that is expected to produce specific character or patterns of behavior especially training that produces moral or mental improvement. From the Latin: *discere,* to learn.

Discipline is also listed as a synonym under punishment, stressing that punishment as a method of training is designed to control an offender and to eliminate or reform unacceptable conduct.

In it's essence, punishment is a penalty, paid with money or *poena.* The connotation is that the person being punished has funds along with knowledge of right and wrong. Does a child fit in that definition?

Discipline with its meaning rooted in learning, has a different significance altogether. Disciples follow their teacher. People, who follow a leader, choose to follow.

The misuse of words can cloud our thinking and dilute meanings so that concepts, such as punishment and discipline, appear to be interchangeable, when in fact they are not.

With a clear understanding of these two ideas, we can ask ourselves, do we want to punish or penalize our children to teach them, or do we want to teach by walking a path that our children can follow, a path down which they can lead others?

Years ago when these two terms were clarified in my mind, I realized punishment was not going to accomplish the teaching I wanted to share with my children. Punishment was not going to promote the learning or self-discipline I hoped to instill.

The question to myself became: How can I best teach my children with this pure idea of discipline? What direction do I want to lead, because it is one that my children will follow? The question was not, "How can I best punish my child?"

To me, Jeff, that is the difference.

There is a place for punishment in our society. It is for those who willingly break established rules or laws. Punishment is for those who willfully endanger others and or their property. It is for those who have attained full rights as citizens. It is for those who are expected to have understanding of societal expectations and consequences. Punishment is designed for those who have resources to pay the penalty or *poena*. This is what reaching a majority age means. Children are not of majority age. Children are minors.

With minors, we are in the process of teaching these children the path they should follow. Our challenge is to lead the whole person—body, mind, heart and spirit. Our challenge is that we must model the self-discipline, the vision, the passion and the conscience that is at the heart of true learning and self-discovery for our children.

When we discipline our children, we walk a path with them of trust, helping them to understand how to live their lives, how to develop their talents, how to share their love and how to do what's right. Corrections on our path should strive to be of loving intention to serve the needs of the child.

Jeff, I hope I've been able to explain the difference between punishment and discipline, so that you can choose the way you want to lead.

Five Dangerous Behaviors

"You must be the change you wish to see in the world." — *Mahatma Mohandas Gandhi*

We have all experienced the person. The person with the negative attitude whose dark cloud metastasizes throughout a relationship, family, business or community, bringing discord, disorder and disaster.

In order to maintain harmonious relationships, Stephen Covey in *The Eighth Habit* says that there are five "cancerous" behaviors we need to stop, not only within ourselves, but also in others.

Complaining. Criticizing. Comparing. Competing. Contending. Five behaviors that destroy relationships.

Complaining. Nothing is ever good enough for the person who complains.

Criticizing. Nobody can ever do anything right for this person.

Comparing. This person compares people or possessions with envy, jealousy or put-downs.

Competing. This person thinks they are better, smarter or richer than everyone else.

Contending. This person tries to make other people look like losers, so he or she can look like a winner. Everything is a competition.

How can we protect our children from developing these attitudes? How can we change negative behaviors?

Be an example of a positive attitude. My nine-year old friend Caiti told me about her first trip to see the Yankees. Caiti described the game-stopping downpour in the 7th inning. "Wow!" she beamed. "Some people have to go to 10 or 20 games before they get to experience a rained-out inning. I got to see it my first time. Can you believe how lucky I am?" Bet you Caiti's ability to make lemonade out of lemons began at home.

Realize negative attitudes signal something deeper is happening. Millicent, an attractive professional salesperson, criticized co-workers' and customers' appearance. Recently divorced, the five cancerous behaviors fed on Millicent's insecurity and damaged self-worth. Among her daily comments—Can you believe her make-up? He's sure a Bozo in that tie. Where did she find those rags?

Millicent's apartment burned to the ground, literally leaving her with only the clothes on her back. All her possessions—make-up, clothes, jewelry, car—gone and uninsured. Customers and co-workers came to her aid, and Millicent understood that there were people who cared for her, no matter what she looked like, or what she had said. Millicent said, "I'll never make another unkind remark about someone. You never know what a person has endured. You have to try to look at the real person. We are all worthy of respect."

Smile and encourage skills. A person's negativity can seem to be beyond our ability to comprehend and change it. The key attributes to effecting positive change in our relationships are to increase knowledge, sharpen skills and alter attitude. We tend to focus on knowledge and attitudes, when focusing on skill development might be the solution.

Six-year-old Allie refused to write. "Everyone can write better than me. Please don't make me write," Allie cried.

Allie's attitude loomed large. So I smiled, and directed Allie to hand strengthening activities. I encouraged her to draw with colored pencils, and to decorate the edges of paper with designs. In a few weeks, her hands developed enough for her to feel successful in writing.

As Allie's skill grew, her outlook improved. In the interim I met her complaints and comparisons with a smile, knowing I could not change her disposition. Focusing on strengthening skills indirectly allowed Allie and me to maintain a harmonious relationship.

When we are up against complaining, criticizing, comparing, competing and contending attitudes, we need to remember to look on the sunny side, seek to understand the root of the behavior, and smile while encouraging new skills.

Addressing Key Frustrations With Your Children

"If life is a bowl of cherries, why am I in the pits?" Erma Bombeck knew how to see the humor in day-to-day reality.

Maintaining a positive and forward moving life is a challenge to say the least. Life has a way of helping us misplace our sense of humor in a hurry. Some days the sailing is smooth with fluffy breezes, while on others we might have to restrain ourselves from self-inflicted baldness.

In our efforts to fix problems, we might be best served by stepping back and examining our frustrations. Instead of trying to affix blame by saying "that's your fault" or "that's my fault," we need to understand why the problem occurred. Let's ask instead, "What is causing this frustration?"

Consider what is going on at the moment you feel frustrated and jot it in a notebook. I used to keep a slip of paper in my pocket to capture those instances then transfer my annoyances to a notebook. These incidents included people being late for appointments, telephone interruptions, spilled foods, children squabbling, stopping an activity to prepare snacks, etc. I'd record the day, time and event in my notebook, and any other issues that I thought might be of value.

Noting these rough spots helped me ascertain the true causes and effects later, as a pattern began to emerge.

After noting problems for a couple of weeks I was able to determine the design of most of my frustrations. Looking at my notes I asked, "Are certain events more common at a certain time of day, on specific days, or with predictable people or activities?"

When I am able to pick out common elements and themes, it becomes clear what needs to change.

When my daughters were about three and four, one of my major frustrations was bedtime. Most nights the girls would go to bed without too many delays.

Except for the nights that my children seemed to have had a cup of espresso for dinner. There were tears about the lights being turned off. They needed a glass of water. Or to go to the bathroom. They were hungry. They wanted another story, another song, another prayer. They were too hot. Too cold. They couldn't find their teddy bear. They heard a strange noise. The neighbor's light bothered them. One of them hit the other one.

On those nights I didn't know what to do. Whatever I did, bedtime was anything but restful, and it felt like it was my fault. Surely, I was doing something wrong.

When I looked over my frustration notebook, I discerned a design. The nights that the girls were reluctant sleepers were the nights that their dad was out of town, back from a trip, had called to tell them goodnight, or arrived home for the evening thirty minutes before bedtime. Ah! Hah! My daughters' nocturnal activities were directed towards trying to secure "daddy time."

Once I saw the pattern, I was able to anticipate my daughters' need for "daddy time" and work with my husband to coordinate phone calls and arrival times. On the nights my husband was out of town, the girls and I spent a few minutes drawing a picture for him, or I'd tell a special "daddy" story.

Looking in my notebook I found that my daughters' disruptions weren't their fault or my fault, or even my husband's fault. I saw that if we couldn't have a bowl of cherries, we could have at least have a "chair of bowlies." We didn't have to settle for the pits.

Seven Traits That Can Destroy Lives

Ever notice how a word, a phrase, a quote, or a book title keeps popping up? Over the past couple of years the following Gandhi quote keeps showing up in my studies. Every time I read these seven statements I am astounded at the wisdom conveyed in so few words.

Gandhi is attributed with saying that these seven characteristics are the most spiritually perilous traits to humanity:

Wealth without work

Pleasure without conscience
Knowledge without character
Commerce without morality
Science without humanity
Worship without sacrifice
Politics without principles

There are natural laws of physics and if we choose to ignore the laws of gravity, thermodynamics, or centrifugal motion, we risk dire consequences. We'll fall, get burned, or be thrown off the merry-go-round.

If we choose to ignore universal principles of human relations, we also put our lives at risk. In these seven lines Gandhi points out that the journey is more important than the destination, and that the means of our activities are as vital as the ends.

Wealth without work. When we don't allow our children to experience the direct result of their labor, or the labor of others, we do them a disservice. Knowing how to sweep and mop a floor gives us an appreciation of a clean floor. A college freshman I know was shocked to learn he had to wash his own clothes. He had never considered, or appreciated, how his clothes appeared clean in his closet. Luxury without understanding the labor that achieved it is a dangerous way to live.

Pleasure without conscience. The by-product of learning is the fun that comes from learning. The reason to learn is in the sheer pleasure of knowing. When we seek pleasure without doing the work of obtaining knowledge, pleasure becomes an unsatisfying deed that can lead us into a life of searching for self-gratification instead of seeking its true source, knowledge.

Knowledge without character. We can be the most knowledgeable person in the world, but if others think we are a jerk and don't want anything to do with us, what good is knowledge? Knowledge is for the benefit of mankind, and without character, it benefits no one.

Commerce without morality. Or business without ethics. If we conduct our work without regards to how it affects the lives of others, we walk on thin ice. A quick read through the *Wall Street Journal* affirms Gandhi's statement.

Science without humanity. Science, the observation of the world in order to create knowledge, needs at its core to be of service to mankind. In the words of Albert Schweitzer, "I don't know what your destiny will be, but one thing I know: the only ones among you who will be really happy are those who will have sought and found how to serve."

Worship without sacrifice. Whatever we value in our lives, whatever we admire, we revere, we love—our families, our children, our spouses, our friends, our planet, our God—we must give these things what they need to survive and thrive. Love and relationships do not exist without the giving of our being.

Politics without principles. We cannot chart a course for our communities without using the laws of universal principles to guide us. How can we otherwise make sure that there is "liberty and justice for all"? Building community requires that we discuss and debate what is fair, respectful, honest, kind, right, trustworthy, responsible, and more. Gandhi warns us that rules not based on sound principles turn to conflict and violence.

As we walk with our children though this adventure called life, let us heed Gandhi's admonitions. As a means to our ends, let us reach our goals guided by universal principles. Because in their hearts of hearts, our children understand that the ends and the means are inseparable.

Misbehavior Meets Needs

Misbehavior. That's when you don't act the way I want you to when I want you to.

But what about when I do what I want when I want to do it? Some might call it personal prerogative. Others might say it's a double standard.

One of the interesting aspects of human behavior is that behavior is need driven. Needs can be physical or spiritual, or perhaps a mixture of both. For example, our need for food fills a physical need, hunger, along with the spiritual needs of belonging, beauty, and more.

As long as we go about filling our needs in culturally appropriate ways, others consider us behaving. As soon as our needs inconvenience someone by creating an obstacle for the fulfillment of their needs…BOOM…our behavior transforms into misbehavior.

For our children, who have not yet learned the cultural nuances of conduct, these crashes and clashes of unmet needs can create disturbances that adults label as misbehavior.

Physical needs are the ones that we usually think of first when we are dealing with a clash of needs between child and adult. Is the child hungry, tired, sleepy, cold, etc.? And perhaps the adults too?

No wonder grandmothers around the world want to feed crabby people. Cookies with milk, along with predictable meal and bedtimes, keep life on an even keel. Taking care of our physical needs avoids considerable conflict.

Meeting spiritual needs becomes trickier and more complex as spiritual needs involve the intellectual, emotional, physical, as well as the spiritual parts of our beings.

Spiritual needs include the following and more: activity, movement, exercise, creativity, exploration, orientation, belonging, acceptance, appreciation, becoming, celebration, closeness, community, consideration, contribution, emotional safety, empathy, honesty, love, reassurance, respect, support, trust, understanding, warmth, communication, inspiration, laughter, fun, imagination, to choose dreams, goals and values, create self worth, create meaning, create an authentic person, create personal integrity, order, beauty, harmony, peace, repetition, precision and exactness.

With so many needs to meet, we all can get needy quickly. We can be going around minding our own business…Ka-Boom! Our needs smash into someone else's.

From a child's point of view, there is no misbehavior, only actions for trying to meet personal needs. Let's look at a few examples.

The child running in the back aisle of the store? Meeting a need for movement and self-expression.

The child giving an adult an imperious, "No!" Meeting a need to become independent.

The child refusing to go to bed? Meeting a need for adult attention.

The child lashing out at friends? Perhaps meeting the need to be alone, to have time to collect thoughts, or the need for protection.

The next time there is a sonic boom in your life, as unmet needs move faster than the speed of sound, think about what unmet needs—yours and your child's—have collided.

Work towards a win-win solution in order for all parties to have their needs met, with no need for misbehaving.

Ain't Misbehavin'

Children don't misbehave, says Dr. Thomas Gordon, author of the best selling book, *Parent Effectiveness Training (P.E.T.)*.

Wait a second, you say. Whoa! Everywhere you look there are children misbehaving.

Dr. Gordon says that children's actions are judged as misbehaviors when those behaviors come into conflict with the desires of parents and other adults. What we judge or perceive to be misbehaviors are actually a child's efforts to have his or her needs met.

For example, three-year-old Stephanie enters her fourteen-year-old sister's room and pours out all of Lisa's make-up and cologne into Lisa's underwear drawer, while applying a new face. Big mess. Big perceived misbehavior. Especially by big sister.

Human beings have many needs, and trying to meet these needs makes us human. We will gain insight into Stephanie's actions, when we look at how Stephanie was trying to meet her needs.

Stephanie's parents, Jim and Linda, analyzed Stephanie's behavior by asking how Stephanie's needs were satisfied by disorganizing Lisa's room. Jim and Linda looked at the following needs: activity, exploration, orientation, order, becoming, belonging, repetition, precision, exactness, communication and imagination. Let's take a closer view at these needs.

Human beings have a need for activity. Stephanie needed an interesting activity to occupy her. What is that saying about idle hands?

People have a need to explore, orient and order our environment. Stephanie had a desire to explore her sister's off-limits room. Stephanie had watched Lisa open bottles and put them back in the drawer, but Stephanie didn't understand the order of the process. Stephanie had a need to orient herself to this grown-up activity.

Humans have a need to become, to have a sense of growth. Stephanie had watched her sister and mother put on make-up. We also have a need to belong. Stephanie wanted to put on make-up due to a need to become and to belong as a female in her family.

People have a need for repetition, exactness and perfection. Lisa should be careful. Because Stephanie didn't get the make-up activity right the first time, Stephanie may have a need to try again, and again.

Stephanie also had a need to communicate she was a "big girl," since there was such an age spread between Lisa and her. Stephanie needed to use her imagination to create that "big girl" image.

Children's misbehavior occurs when children's actions to meet their needs conflict with adult's needs. To meet everyone's needs, both children's and adults, Dr. Gordon recommends that we step out of our roles as parents and focus on being a person, a human being who has needs, who is trying to help another younger and smaller person meet his or her needs. It's about finding a solution where everyone wins.

Jim and Linda made it clear to Stephanie that Lisa's room was off limits, but also designed some activities that helped meet Stephanie's needs. Lisa put together a basket of small colored bottles that Stephanie could open and close. Linda made Stephanie a mirrored make-up kit of lotions. Lisa kept her door locked but also spent time with Stephanie, letting her put make-up on Lisa.

By considering Stephanie's behavior as need driven, Jim, Linda, and Lisa found a way to direct Stephanie's activities so that both Stephanie's needs and their adult need for order (and sanity) could be met.

For more information about Parent Effectiveness Training, visit www.gordontraining.com/familyresources.html

BELLS
Communicating and Connecting

ach cathedral has a distinctive set of bells that ring out to communicate the passing of events. Bells tolled on the hour, on the birth or death of a community member, or in emergencies.

In Florence we planned to be at the Boboli Garden by noon in order to hear the bells toll all over the city. What a glorious sound it was to listen to a city full of music.

In Sienna we were near the bell tower at noon and the sound tended more towards cacophony than music. Later we climbed up the bell tower along narrow stairs to see the bells. All I could think of is how oppressing it must be to have the job of bell ringer. The cramped space, the deafening noise, the unmelodious clang.

From a distance, the bells' tones are like the "music of the spheres." But does a bell ringer ever know how many people find beauty and peace in the fruit of his labors?

As parents and teachers we are bell ringers. We are responsible for communicating and connecting our children to their world. The work is hard, anonymous, and unappreciated. Plus, it can give you a huge headache.

Once in a while we need to distance ourselves so that we can appreciate and understand our work. We need to stop and listen to the bells and know their heavenly sounds toll for us, and that we are part of a magnificent symphony.

Forgive and Forget

"Forgive and forget" is a phrase that is given as advice. As a child, I remember being upset over a transgression and yelling, "I don't want to forgive her, and I won't forget it!" Forgive and forget seemed to mean that I should pardon the misdeed and pretend it never happened. That, in my mind, just wasn't right.

When a neighbor girl pushed me down, causing me to skin my knees, and proceeded to take my Popsicle money, it seemed plain stupid to pardon the grievance and pretend it had never happened. Surely I needed to remember the incident so I could protect myself from it happening again. Pardon the grievance? Taking my Popsicle money was stealing. All I knew was that stealing was on the list of don'ts for the Ten Commandments. These were ten things that God didn't want us to forget, so how could I? This is the way I saw it when I was six-years-old.

As I've had children of my own and taught school, I've learned that hurt occurs one of two ways: accidentally or intentionally. We need to help our children be prepared to deal with the inevitable in their lives.

Accidents hurt as much as an intentional wound. I've taught my preschool students that when an accident occurs, they have responsibilities. If they are hurt, they need to let the others involved know, as well as what they need to remedy the situation, as it may not be apparent. For example, "I hurt my knee. Can you get me a bandage?"

If their actions caused an accident, I coached students to offer an apology. By ignoring the incident and not apologizing, they ran the risk of people thinking they acted with intent. The sooner an apology is offered, the better. Between the ages of three to six, children are in a critical period for learning social skills, so showing them how to apologize can be done in a matter of fact way.

An apology consists of four steps. First, say you're sorry. Secondly, ask how to help the other person get back to normal or feel better. Next, offer to change behavior so the incident doesn't reoccur. Finally, ask for the apology to be accepted. A sincere apology might sound like this:

"I'm so sorry. I didn't mean to run into you. Are you hurt? How can I help you? I'll be more careful about where I'm going. Will you accept my apology?"

Being accidentally hurt by a person who expresses concern about you can be forgiven and forgotten. Most of the hurts of a three to six-year-old are accidental. As we get older, unfortunately, we need to learn to deal with those who intended to harm us.

With intentional aggression, we need to teach a deeper interpretation of "forgive and forget." Our elementary age children will deal with people taking their possessions, name calling, physical threats and more. As adults, we may have to deal with the person who robs our house, the coworker that lies and gossips about us, or the con artist who embezzles our savings. Unremorseful people, who hurt us intentionally, are hard to forget about and forgive.

It's easy to fall into the trap of wanting to hurt those who have hurt us. We want to avenge ourselves and prove they are wrong. Wanting to get even can consume us and rob us of enjoying our lives. We all know of people who have spent years trying to get even. They couldn't forget about the incident or forgive it. If they had known how, they could have recovered and gotten on with their lives. Isn't this what we want for our children?

Forgive is an old word, from the Old English "give forth." Give forth what? Love. To heal our wounds, we must "give forth" love to our aggressor. Just as we can't expect orange juice from a lemon, we can't expect people who feel unloved to show love to others.

There are stories of people "forgiving" the murderers of loved ones. "Giving forth" love was the beginning of the healing process for the survivors. The forgiven murderers also began to feel remorse and heal as they experienced, probably for the first time in their lives, the power of love and forgiveness. The wrong doer is not pardoned. He still has to suffer the consequences of his actions. His actions are not condoned. The process of "giving forth" love by forgiving releases victim and perpetrator from a downward spiral of revenge and hatred. Forgiving helps them heal and regain a peaceful life.

Forgiving is a gift to ourselves because it lets us heal and reclaim our lives. We also need to forget. To forget, we have to "get forth" and move forward with our lives and not be consumed with revenge or hatred. If we don't move forward, and continue to dwell on the injustices of the past, we will be stuck in a morass of hatred, and lose the joyfulness of our lives.

To help our children, we need to remember the old phrase, forgive and forget. "Give forth love and get forth with life." It is not about pardoning and ignoring wrongdoing. It is a time-tested adage to help us live a life filled with love and joy, and experience the power of living in the now.

Giving Thanks: Cultivating an Attitude of Gratitude

"What do you see?" our communications professor asked as he held up a black and white ink drawing.

"A beautiful Gibson-style girl with a feather in her hat."

"No, it's an old hag with a witch's nose and a scarf tied over her head."

As we discussed this picture, most of the class could shift back and forth and see both images by directing our attention to one aspect of the drawing until our perception changed. Once we saw both figures, it seemed easy to move between them. We realized that the pretty and the ugly were imbedded in the picture. What we saw depended on where we put our attention.

What a valuable lesson that picture has been for me in seeing the positive. The other lesson, much harder to learn, is that the "not-so-positive" resides in every picture or situation. It's wise to search for the down side as protection against negativity.

Striving for that delicate balance of optimism, pessimism and realism challenges me. An optimist sees the glass as half full. The pessimist sees it as half empty. The realist says, "Someone's going to have to get water."

If we focus on the negative, we can get into a "crabby habit of mind" as Dr. John Gottman warns in his book, *The Relationship Cure*. With all the worries we have in our lives—children, spouse, jobs, family, etc.—it can take a concentrated effort to shift our perception to the positive, the beautiful, the good and the thankful in our relationships. To refocus, we need to count our blessings.

Dr. Gottman encourages us to exercise Thanksgiving every day by expressing gratitude and thanks to those around us. When we are too focused on the negative Dr. Gottman recommends giving thanks as a cure for the crabby habit of mind. When we find ourselves being overly critical of our loved ones, we can shift our focus by finding reasons to value them. Even though we might feel our criticism is justified, Gottman recommends finding and sharing five bits of praise and appreciation daily with the people who earned it.

Three-year-old Penelope couldn't do anything right. Penelope threw puzzles, walked over others' work, made hurtful remarks, and stuck out her tongue with disrespect. After visiting with Penelope's mother and father about her behavior, we decided to shift our focus and find some quality or task that we could appreciate and share with her. For example, "Penelope, I saw how you hung up your coat on a hangar this morning."

As long as no safety issues were broached, her classroom teacher remained quiet with any criticism of Penelope's behavior and focused on the positive. As the days went by we shared with Penelope "bits of praise and appreciation" when she earned it. In two weeks, Penelope's behavior had changed dramatically, and she exhibited none of her previous actions. One classroom observer didn't believe Penelope was the same child.

Dr. Gottman lists about 75 qualities we can find to appreciate and praise. Some of these follow: loving, intelligent, strong, energetic, persistent, funny, gentle, kind, relaxed, beautiful, calm, tender, careful, strong, interesting and helpful.

If you find yourself in a "crabby habit of mind," shift your focus to the blessing instead of the criticism. Look for the positive, knowing full well the negative is there. Find qualities to appreciate and praise. What you feed grows, so feed positive qualities with appreciation and ignore negative qualities as long as no one is hurt. As you find qualities to be thankful for in your children and others, you will cultivate an attitude of gratitude. May every day be a day of thanksgiving for you and yours.

When All Else Fails, Sing

The dot on my hand darkened to black, deep black.

Wearing a plastic mood dot was part of my stress management class. If all went well, the dot shone blue. If not, it turned shades of bluish-black, to midnight.

In my preschool class, over the course of a couple of weeks, I noticed that certain events and activities turned my dot black—events that most moms and dads face multiple times a day.

Transition times. Transition times headed up my list of stressful moments. Moving from one activity to another, such as work time to lunchtime, lunch to recess, recess back to class and dismissals. Most parents report that going from one event to another, for example, getting dressed then on to breakfast, breakfast to school, school to home, bath to bed, reign as the times of day that their "black dot" appears.

Another black dot instant coincided with those unpredictable moments that we have with children where everything can be calm and peaceful, then in a blink of an eye, change to chaos for no apparent reason.

Determined to figure out how to create blue dot moments, I kept a daily log. When I was actively involved giving lessons, reading a book out loud, or singing, the mood dot was blue skies. During interruptions, phone calls, and transition times storm clouds brewed across my dot, and I felt my impatience and grumpiness emerge.

Deciding to follow the advice of the old song, "accentuate the positive, eliminate the negative," I determined to use my blue-sky activities to full advantage, and try to eliminate that stormy weather.

Interruptions and phone calls I minimized by setting limits. For transition times, I ventured to find a song or two for each changeover of activity. As we sang while changing activities, I noted that my mood dot stayed blue, and could changed from black to blue in less than thirty-seconds.

In moments of chaotic classroom meltdown, when it would have been easier to yell, "Please be quiet," I sang. Serendipitously, I found that when I sang in another language, the group quieted in seconds. I busied myself learning several songs in Spanish and German. My one Chinese song, though, consistently calms any preschool group. How? Developing language in preschoolers creates a fascination for new words, and they will stop to listen to something unfamiliar.

For transition times, I used songs such as *Mary Wore Her Red Dress* and *Willabee Wallaby Wee* to dismiss children one by one to a new activity. There were songs for clean up time (One, two, three, four, five, six, seven, eight, nine, let's finish up, it's clean up time). For lunch, we sang, "This is the way we get ready for lunch."

These songs helped create a routine, along with relieving my stress, and the children's tension. Newcomers to the classroom adapted quickly with musical cues to aid in their assimilation. Expectations become clear with our musical routine.

Here's wishing you blue-sky dots and days. Remember, when things start to get you down, sing.

The Power of Family Stories

Every family, every college, every corporation, every institution needs tribal storytellers. The penalty for failing to listen is to lose one's history, one's historical context, one's binding values.—Max DePree, Leadership is an Art

On Christmas Eve, the cousins chose to watch *The Sound of Music*. This surprised me, as the cousins' ages range from pre-teen to twenty-somethings. Within a few minutes, though, three generations were engrossed in a musical that might not be considered cool or masculine.

But what a powerful story. A family making a decision to leave a home and country that they dearly loved. A father having the courage to know that "flight" instead of "fight" was essential for the survival of his family. Through their story, we know the values that the Von Trapps considered vital, and the price they were willing to pay to live by their standards.

Each of us, every family, has stories that communicate the essence of who we are, what we stand for, and how we've survived tough times. We need to find these stories and use them.

Evelyn Clark, author of *Around the Corporate Campfire*, coaches business leaders to use their stories to inspire success in their company, and to communicate values and expectations.

David Armstrong of Armstrong International loves to tell the story of "The Day I Paid $248,000 to Play a Round of Golf." Doesn't that make some of our mistakes look, well, small?

David Armstrong's assistant general manager made a decision to purchase equipment for the cost of $248,000, while his boss was out on the golf course one morning. The manager was authorized to spend $20,000. Even though his manager had gone twelve times over his spending limit, Armstrong didn't fire this employee.

Why? Because the manager took the initiative to buy machines he knew would be needed when the supplier called with an offer for almost new equipment. When the manager learned that another company was interested, he made an on the spot decision. His decisiveness saved Armstrong International significant money, enabled them to catch up on a backlog of orders, and provided better customer service.

That's why David Armstrong loves to tell his $248,000 golf story. It communicates his values. Armstrong uses this story to celebrate decision-making and risk-taking abilities within his organization.

Stories can be powerful teaching tools for our families. We have tales that can help our children understand who we are, who they are, our expectations for them, and how our family meets adversity.

You might think you don't have a history as powerful as the Von Trapp or Armstrong stories, but you do. Each of us has vital experiences we need to explore, tell and retell.

How do we find these stories? Begin by thinking about some of these ideas:

1. What was one of your most embarrassing moments? How did you act? How did you overcome it?

2. What was your happiest moment? How long did it last? How do you retain or recreate that happiness?

3. What was your saddest moment?

4. When did you make a bad decision? What were the consequences? How did you work through the consequences?

Our stories can help our children learn to be resilient, honest, courageous, compassionate, strong, resourceful, and more. Powerful stories tell about deeply held beliefs, an individual's philosophy of life and mission, thus giving a reason for being.

The story of Odysseus in Homer's *The Odyssey* remains a classic because the myth addresses beliefs, philosophy and mission. Odysseus' decisions, good and bad, create life-threatening predicaments. In the original cliffhanger, Odysseus survives to return home, only to discover more difficulties.

To understand how a story communicates convictions, the Puffin Classic version of *The Odyssey* is a worthwhile out loud family read. We are on an odyssey, an amazing adventure. Let's tell tales to convey our family's history, context and values.

Finding Seeds of Appreciation and Gratitude

In our worst traits lay the seeds of our best traits.

In those moments when we criticize behavior, we have an opportunity. If we take the time to shift our perception and look for the positive in the situation, we will find a quality to appreciate.

In those moments when we might be critical, we can make a conscious choice to react to the world in a different way. Instead of feeling irritable and angry while looking for evidence to justify our feelings, we can ask ourselves, "What can I appreciate in this situation? What am I thankful for? How can I express my gratitude?"

Our criticism of others sometimes reflects our intolerance of our own shortcomings.

Pet peeves. We all have them. We can either feed our pet peeves or delve into these annoyances to discover the seeds of a positive trait.

Being hit with a grocery cart in the checkout line used to be one of my pet peeves. Pushy people inching their carts closer and closer in the narrow aisle as my groceries moved toward the cashier drove me crazy. Bumping me more than once as I attempted to write a check was the ultimate annoyance.

As I pushed my bags to the car, I inwardly fumed, "Can you believe that person! Who does he think he is? Why couldn't he keep his cart back ten inches for ten more seconds! Harrumph!"

In some of my studies I came across the idea that perhaps I was critical of my fellow shopper because he reflected my own impatience. My pet peeves were me, reflected back to me. Very interesting.

Next shopping trip, I resolved to be more patient, and to not to be in a hurry to get out of the store. As part of my experiment, I offered my place in line to the person behind me. "Please go next. I'm not in a hurry."

The person following me, instead of pushing their cart forward, stayed a respectful distance back. The shopper in front of me expressed appreciation and kindness.

After this venture, instead of feeling like a bruised and harassed shopper, I left the store feeling kind and appreciated by the other folks in line.

In this way, I discovered that one of my less desirable characteristics, impatience, held the seed to one of my finer traits, kindness.

In our criticism of our children, let us look at their behavior in such a way so that we can discover the seed of their positive features or strengths.

When we see messiness, perhaps we can look for creativity, spontaneity, or imagination and appreciate those qualities.

When we think our children are rude, perhaps we might see the seeds of assertiveness, shyness, expressiveness, or honesty, and help them express those qualities in a positive manner.

When we are irritated by noise or constant requests for attention from our children, let us consider appreciating their lovingness, their energy, their enthusiasm, their strength and their humor.

Look for the seeds of positive qualities at those times when you might be thinking, "Why, oh why, does he have to do that!"

Here are a few positive qualities where you might consider placing your appreciation: Energetic, Honest, Loyal, Intelligent, Brave, Sensitive, Thoughtful, Cheerful, Gracious, Playful, Caring, Exciting, Committed, Active, Adventurous, Responsible, Reliable, Resourceful, Athletic, Funny, Calm, Assertive, Understanding, Creative, Affectionate, Interesting, Honest, Kind, Friendly, Protective, Gentle, Generous, Strong, Coordinated, Graceful, Diligent, Trustworthy.

Research shows that giving people five bits of honest and earned appreciation per day creates strong and supportive relationships. Next time you feel critical, take the time to identify the finer qualities that are hidden in the situation.

Express your appreciation for these traits with a simple thank you. Remember, the seed we feed grows.

Be the Story Teller for Your Child's Special Moments

Erle Stanley Gardner. Agatha Christie. Dick Francis. I've always loved reading mysteries and I've read so many that I can usually guess "who dunnit."

In my late teens I took a writing seminar with a mystery writer. My first question to her was "Do you know the ending when you start writing?" She laughed and said the only way you can write a mystery is to know the ending before you start. Mystery stories, the author told me, are written backwards. You have to know how they end.

Our children though do not have the imaginations or experience to see how their stories are going to end. Our children have no idea of how their little adventures will fit together to create a big story. As parents and as adults in a child's life, we are the keepers of those special moments. We have the job of helping our children see who they are and who they can be. Our job is to tell stories that make life less a mystery and more an adventure.

It is in the telling and retelling of stories that help our children learn to use their imaginations to see how their story might end. We need to tell anecdotes not just about our children but also about the world around them.

It's our choice. We can either tell the stories that help our children see themselves as courageous, caring and responsible human beings, or we can tell them other kinds of stories where the endings are not as hopeful.

It's easy to let the positive stories about our children slip away. Yet, there are tales everyday that can be told, and tales that our children need to hear.

Our nighttime ritual when the girls were preschoolers was for me to tell them the story of our day. It was a perfect time to recount the positive events of the day. I'd start our story of the day with getting out of bed, having breakfast, getting ready for school, the car ride to school, riding home from school, lunch, the books we read in the afternoon, snacks, dinner, getting ready for bed. It was an ideal opportunity to interject events that stood out.

I'd describe what I'd seen, how I felt, and try to sum it up with a word.

"Dana had her shoes and coat on and was helping Hannah as I walked downstairs this morning. It felt good to be ready to go to school a little early this morning. Dana was really *organized* this morning, wasn't she?"

"Kitty and Nicole came over to play. Dana pushed Kitty is the swing and showed her how to pump her legs. Hannah helped get snacks ready for everybody. I think you were both *kind and considerate.*"

"Hannah set the table for dinner. Placemats, napkins, forks, knives, spoons, plates and water glasses. It felt good to see the table ready for dinner. Hannah did a lot of *work.*"

Our children do not have the imagination and experience to know what actions they are doing that will help them become a bigger better person. They do not know enough to imagine where they should be or could be headed. The world will tell our children what's wrong with them. Our job is to let our children know what is right with them. Tell your children how each special moment ends. Don't let it be a mystery.

Giving Sincere Praise

One of the formative experiences of my early twenties was taking the Dale Carnegie Course in Public Speaking and Human Relations. Each class we focused on a tenet of Carnegie's philosophy, one of which is to give sincere, honest appreciation.

But giving honest and sincere appreciation can be a difficult skill to master. Some compliments come across as hints to past mishaps. Someone saying "You look pretty in that outfit," can give the fleeting thought of what might have been left unspoken, such as, "...not like the outfit you had on yesterday."

A compliment can sound manipulative. "You really do an outstanding job cooking wonderful dinners," can contain a hidden message of "...and I think I can get out of helping clean up the kitchen and ever preparing a meal myself if I lay the charm on thick."

Praise can sound over-enthusiastic. "You're just a wonderful artist. Your stuff should hang in the Louvre," may communicate that the speaker may want to push us in a direction we don't care to go.

How can we give sincere, honest appreciation? Dale Carnegie suggested that we bring with us some basic attitudes such as being genuinely interested in other people, smiling, remembering that a person's name is the sweetest sound in any language, being a good listener, talking in terms of the other person's interests instead of your own, and making the other person feel important.

We can give a sincere compliment by describing instead of evaluating. Evaluating type of praise is when we put a value on something. "That is so beautiful. You're so good. That's better than yesterday."

Descriptive compliments describe what you see, what you feel, and then use a word that sums up the entire experience.

Let's use the example of a child cleaning up his or her room. A descriptive compliment might go like this:

Describe what you see. Susan, I see all your books on your shelves. I see all your clothes put away. I see your bed is nice and neat.

Describe what you feel. Susan, it feels wonderful to walk into such an organized room.

Sum up the experience with a word. You worked to get your room looking just so. Susan, that's what I'd call *persistence*.

A descriptive compliment is effective in communicating that we take a genuine interest in our children's efforts, and even more so if we smile, use their name several times, and help our children feel important by summing up the experience in one significant word. (P.S. Descriptive compliments work at the office, with spouses, and other family members.)

Anybody can say "Good job!" It takes a few minutes of thought and genuine interest to show sincere appreciation.

Be prepared for a lot of repetition of any activity that you praise. Be careful to not compliment something that you do not want repeated. Saying "You can really play that xylophone," might lead to a weeklong marathon playing of "Hot Cross Buns."

Sincere appreciation is powerful. Handle with care.

Modeling Behavior

The telephone rang as we sat down for dinner. I excused myself to answer the call.

"Good evening. Is Mrs. Schmidt in, please?" I recognized the voice immediately. It was a telemarketer from a local nonprofit organization where I had ordered five-year guaranteed light bulbs. For months the same two ladies had informed me of their establishment's needs and I purchased light bulbs for every socket in the house, given a few to our neighbors, and stored a half dozen backups in the basement.

My comments about having enough light bulbs didn't deter these sales women. The calls continued, but I didn't want to talk to the light bulb ladies. It usually took me ten minutes to politely disengage myself from a call.

"No," I replied. "She's not here."

"Do you know when she'll be back?"

"No. I don't know when she'll be back. Goodbye."

As I sat back down to dinner, my husband asked me who was on the phone.

"The five-year light bulb people. They won't leave me alone."

"Well," Mark said. "Do you realize you just compromised your integrity to your children?"

It felt like a sledgehammer had hit me in the face. In my desire to be non-confrontational and not to be rude, I had lied. Right in front of my three- and four-year-old daughters. As cool as you please.

What slippery slope had I slithered? There was manure in the barnyard and I was right in the middle of it.

My inability to be truthful and honest to the caller had compromised my principles. Why did I find it impossible to give any of a number of honest messages, such as: Excuse me. We are sitting down to dinner. I can't talk to you. Or—Thank you for calling. I have all the light bulbs I need for the next fifty years. Good-bye. Or—I could have been flat out rude and hung up the phone.

But for whatever reasons, I had found it easier to fib. A white lie, a polite lie, but a falsehood, nonetheless. Casual deceit was not something I wanted to pass down to my children. It was true confession time.

"What I just did was wrong. I should have told the lady on the phone that I didn't want to buy anymore light bulbs or that I was busy with dinner. I didn't want to hurt the sales lady's feelings. I didn't want her to think I was mean and rude. But it is better to have the person on the phone think I'm rude than to have my family think I'm a liar."

Our actions illuminate who we are. From my embarrassment I realized that I needed to choose my words carefully. I learned that in awkward situations there is a way to be honest, yet direct and kind. This was critical as I became uncomfortably aware of how my actions and words could influence my children and impact their perception of acceptable conduct.

That evening, dealing with my little white lie and my humiliation, I uncovered a fundamental truth: Whatever you do, intentional or not, lights a path for your children. Make sure you're headed in the right direction.

Noise Surrounds Us

Blaise Pascal, the 17th century philosopher and mathematician, wrote, "All man's miseries derive from not being able to sit quietly in a room alone."

Almost three hundred years later and human misery still stems from not being able to listen to oneself think. A recent edition of *Ode* magazine was dedicated to the topic of silence. Several journalists detailed their journey into being alone and quiet. One writer found being in a sensory deprivation unit not quiet at all, but disturbingly noisy, as he listened to his heartbeat, his pulse beat in his ears, and paid attention to his breathing. What each traveler into the quiet world found is that there is no silence. Noise surrounds us.

Sitting quietly with our thoughts and listening to our inner being is unsettling at first. How easy it is to distract ourselves. Turn on the television, the computer, and the video game. Pick up the phone, or our music devices. Open the refrigerator door hunting for something because we feel hungry not for food, but for the quiet.

Paying attention to our inner sensations of feeling, hearing, seeing and thinking takes focus and concentration. Sitting quietly alone is the key to discovering where and who we are in the universe. It's much easier to party that to sit and open the package. What a gift we have though when we can sit, as Pascal suggests, alone in a room and not feel lonely.

Our world today is filled with more distractions than in Pascal's time, distractions that help us avoid direct confrontation of who we are. We let "noise" distract us from our dreams, our desires, and ultimately our lives, because we fear hearing our breath, our heartbeat, and the blood rush through our ears.

Only in the quiet can we listen to that voice that coaches us to be the person we were meant to be. If only there weren't so much noise.

Today take five minutes to listen to your breathing and to your heartbeat. Listen to your dreams. Tomorrow listen for another five minutes. Listen everyday until you are quiet for twenty minutes a day.

"Learn to be silent. Let your quiet mind listen and absorb," Pythagoras recommended over 2500 years ago.

Sit comfortably in a room alone and your children, and others around you, will be affected by the concentric waves of peace and quiet that you create.

In today's world our children are at risk for never having the opportunity to learn to sit quietly. Movement is crucial to child development, but being still and quiet is also of vital import. Without a sense of direction, movement is misguided. Without movement, inspiration is never fulfilled.

What are those things that keep our children from having quiet time? Take a few minutes and make a list of all those activities that prevent quiet from being in your family's life. Television. Radio. Computers. Personal music devices. Cell phones. Video games. Over scheduling.

Don't let the noise of life prevent your children from having the opportunity to listen to themselves, and discover who they are.

Children Love Quiet

Somehow between Madison Avenue and Hollywood, and all the places where kiddie culture is fed, we're given the view that children are rowdy and eternally needing to be entertained.

Picture a scene of children getting out from school. What do you imagine? More than likely it's children shouting and running from the school building.

Though the movies would have us believe otherwise, children actually love quiet.

The portrayal of children in our popular culture tends to over emphasize hyperactivity and hyper-noise. Children require movement and appropriate, yet creative, methods to express themselves, which unfortunately, are not readily given. If we, as adults, had to do what some children must everyday, we'd be portrayed as running out of buildings screaming at the top of our lungs.

Our world is a noisy place and most of us haven't learned how to move softly through space. Years ago after a function in our church fellowship hall, the volunteer clean up crew began to drag chairs and tables across the room in order to place them in storage racks. The rumble deafened. Screeching metal legs against the linoleum made chalkboards and fingernails seem melodic.

My daughters covered their ears, wondering out loud, "Why don't they carry the chairs quietly?"

"Because," I said, "I don't think anybody's shown them how."

My daughters looked at each other quizzically. As if on cue they each picked up an end of a table and carried it across the room. As they moved across the floor, the noisy volunteers stopped to see youngsters carrying a six-foot table, quietly. Very quietly indeed.

Our children love quiet, but as the church volunteers demonstrated, we neglect to show them how to move quietly, how to appreciate the quiet, and how to listen.

Children enjoy a listening game where everyone gets quiet for about two minutes, which is a very long time for three and four-year-olds, and for some 34-year-olds, too. I'd set an hourglass type egg timer in the middle of our group to give the children a focal point and concept of how much longer they should sit and listen. In the quiet the children heard each other sigh, squirm, and change positions. In short the children became aware of how a simple movement disrupts the mood of the group. At the end of the two minute period I would go around the group and ask each child what they heard as they listened.

Without exception, the children were amazed what they could hear. Birds outside even though all the doors and windows were shut. Cars at the stop sign a block away. A fire truck leaving the station a mile away. The rumble of a train. The neighbor's tractor or leaf blower. The refrigerator. The heat clicking on. The air going through their noses. The clock ticking in the adjoining room. The faucet dripping in the bathroom. In the quiet the children listened.

After this five to ten minute listening exercise the children appeared more confident and controlled in their actions, left the group lesson with a tranquil smile, and worked rest of the morning with deeper concentration than before the lesson.

Children love quiet. All they need is to learn how to listen and to be heard. Just like the rest of us.

Building Cathedrals Not Walls

WINDOWS
Revealing the Child's True Nature

---

lassmakers started work on the stained glass windows as the roof of the cathedral was being finished. Cathedral glass was made from molten sand and ash with the addition of certain metals to create color. Stained glass artists cut and pieced together glass to create windows up to 60 feet high.

For many of us the windows in a cathedral seem to be the reason for the cathedral. The beauty and light of the windows seem to lift the eyes and spirit to higher thoughts.

In many ways inner development is an intricate and hidden process much like the building of a stained glass window. Until all the pieces of a window are cut and in place, the window's beauty cannot be conceived. Until our children's inner development is revealed, we may be left in the dark about who are children are. It is our children's inner development that allows their personalities to shine through. The interesting idea is that our children are creating themselves, building their personalities with the experiences in their environment.

Our children come to us as spiritual embryos, beings at work to build themselves. From birth, children have an inner life. Human development is a lengthy and internal process—a puzzling process that produces unpredictable results.

For each of us, our inner development could be likened to the building of a stained glass window. It is a fragile process with intricate detail that ends with amazing results. More astonishing, is that the child is the builder of this stained glass window of personality that rest of the world will see.

In a cathedral the ability to place the window depends on the strength of the foundation, columns and walls, the protection of the roof, and the deflection of rain by the gargoyles. The child's inner development depends on the structures of love, family and work, character development, protection from physical and psychological harm, as well as overcoming developmental obstacles and meeting needs.

At some point, the child's inner being shines like a Rose Window comprised of thousands of pieces of molten crystal reflecting a unique personality. Dazzling.

Understanding Your Child's Artwork

A visitor gushed over my four-year-old daughter's new and quite abstract painting on our refrigerator. "Oh, what a beautiful painting. It's the most beautiful thing I've ever seen."

I was pleased that my daughter had remembered to say thank you to a compliment. I thought she would also enjoy the "non-mom" appreciation. After our visitor was gone, my daughter turned to me and said, "That lady sure doesn't know anything about art. I guess she's never been to a museum. It's not the most beautiful picture in the world. It's just a picture I did about trains."

That's the day I learned that a four-year-old can spot a phony compliment. It's also the day that I discovered that blobs and scribbles may actually contain an important story.

"So your picture is about trains. Tell me about it." I had been amazed that the picture was about anything. It resembled the drop cloth of a messy house painter.

"This is the train we saw with all the circus animals on it. Here is the yellow engine and here is the green caboose."

At least six weeks before we had stopped to watch the Ringling Brothers train roll through town. The train had a yellow Santa Fe engine and a green Burlington Northern caboose. I hadn't realized she remembered any of it.

"What's the blue here?" I said.

"That's the car with the elephants."

On and on she went about the day we saw the circus train. I was delighted by the detail she remembered and had expressed in her painting. I thought of her other "artwork" I had thrown away. So many stories I tossed out because I didn't ask a few questions. I just didn't know.

This incident with my daughter taught me to ask open-ended questions about artwork. Instead of some "Oh, how nice!" compliment, I've learned to approach children's artwork with phrases such as, "Tell me about your picture. What is this red? Tell me about the yellow. What is the blue about?" I also include the famous five questions of who, what, when, where, and why. Who was there? What did they do? When did this happen? Where did this happen? Why were you there? These questions have helped me understand the story inside a picture.

With these few questions, I hope you'll discover something new about your child. Splotches of color on a piece of brown craft paper let me experience something that was important to my daughter. With her drawing, she was able to share with me a memory of an important event in her life. Her refrigerator artwork became one of the most beautiful pictures I had ever seen, because I took the time to try to understand the artist.

To Foster Cooperation, Give Choices

Most of the conflict we have with our preschool age children involves getting them to do something they don't want to do in a reasonable amount of time. Eating, getting dressed, going to bed, or taking a bath may be familiar conflict areas. In parenting class, I was introduced to the idea of giving choices to avoid conflict. When we give choices, or freedom within limits, we can help our children feel in control of themselves, foster cooperation and develop independence.

How and when to present choices is critical to the success of implementing this concept. If we give too many choices, we may create an environment of frustration and again encounter non-cooperation. Giving too few choices, we risk being authoritarian, and may create rebellion or subterfuge in our children. The art of implementation is looking at each child and situation with fresh and understanding eyes, while remaining kind and firm.

Everyday was a struggle to brush my two-and-a-half-year-old's teeth. Hannah lacked the fine motor control to do the job alone and resisted mightily when I tried. I was totally frustrated and bedtime was a disaster. At our dental check up I mentioned to Dr. Jim about our brushing conflict.

"Hannah," Dr. Jim said. "Why are you fighting with your mom about brushing your teeth?"

"The toothpaste burns my mouth."

"Let's try some different flavors. I have cinnamon, bubblegum, peppermint, and strawberry. Which one do you want to taste first?"

Hannah cheerfully sampled each flavor and selected a tube. That was the end of our Battle of the Brush. I remain thankful to Dr. Jim for lowering my stress level twenty points with bubblegum flavored toothpaste. I hadn't considered giving Hannah a choice of toothpaste. I hadn't even thought to ask her why she was upset.

Years later, I witnessed my friend, Martha, go overboard with choices.

"Jimmy would you like oatmeal or eggs for breakfast?"

"Oatmeal."

Do you want blueberry, strawberry, cinnamon or maple flavor?"

"Cinnamon."

"Do you want brown sugar or honey?"

"Honey."

"Do you want butter or milk on it?"

"Milk."

Do you want it in the white or the blue bowl? Do you want apple, grape or orange juice?"

Poor Jimmy. This two-year-old was interrogated for breakfast. After the third question I watched Jimmy's eyes glaze. When the blue bowl arrived, Jimmy gave his mother "a look" and dumped his oatmeal on the table. "Giving choices just isn't working," Martha lamented.

Giving too many choices doesn't work, is what I observed. Martha should have stopped at oatmeal!

Question after question turned a picky eater into a rebel. When a child is defiant, he is asking us, "Who is the boss here? You act like it's me. If it's you, then show me."

Don't be afraid of showing your child that defiant behavior is unacceptable. He is asking for limits to be set and enforced. Too many choices can cause a child to question his role in the parent/child relationship. Our children need for us to be the adult in charge, so they can feel safe and secure.

We also need to be on guard for giving choices that aren't appropriate. Dawn thought that giving her four-year-old daughter, Sophie, a choice about what time to go to bed would make bedtime smoother. In reality, bedtime was not negotiable for Dawn, as Sophie thought her choice was no bedtime. Chaos and unhappiness ensued. Dawn realized she needed to set and enforce bedtime. The choices Dawn gave Sophie were decisions such as what color pajamas to wear, what books to read, and what prayers to say. When Dawn set the limits regarding time, and gave Sophie freedom within those limits, bedtime became calmer. Sophie understood her limits and the freedom she had within those limits. Bedtime became a loving ritual instead of a power struggle.

Allowing choices fosters self-control, cooperation and independence in our children. Be aware of giving too many or inappropriate choices. When your child gets to those bumpy teenage years, he or she will have many years of practicing making "good" choices. You'll be able to feel confident in your teenager's ability to continue to make "good" choices when dealing with tough decisions with friends, drugs and alcohol.

The Child In Nature

There are two spiritual dangers in not owning a farm. One is the danger of supposing that breakfast comes from the grocery, and the other that heat comes from the furnace.—Aldo Leopold, A Sand County Almanac, 1949

A visit to a toy store in a California beach town uncovered a new product, a mud pie kit. The packaging information offered that the dirt was sterilized, just add water. Plastic bowl, molds and spoons included. Holding this package, selling for fifteen dollars, I felt a deep sadness for the child who would use this plaything.

One of my gifts is my clear memories from age two. How many happy hours and afternoons I spent digging in the side yard, making mud creations decorated with leaves, sticks, mulberries and stones, while sitting on a coveted flat rock or brick.

On summer afternoons, the east side of the house would be cool and shaded, populated with rollie-pollies and an occasional June bug. Evenings were spent in the back yard chasing lightening bugs, waiting for the sky to darken enough to see the Milky Way after a vibrant red and purple sunset, serenaded by cicadas. Mornings we were out chasing bumblebees in the clover.

Spring afternoons we discovered the first crocuses, daffodils and tulips, pussy willow, forsythias, and, my mother's favorite, asparagus. As we dug under the blossoming plum, the tree hummed with the pollen collection of bees.

Autumn leaves were used to make mountains, forts and jumping piles. Spying the stars from the back of the car, the Big Dipper seemed to point the way home from my grandparents on winter evenings.

My earliest recollections are of my interaction with nature. These are calm and peaceful memories, the one's I reach for when I seek solace. The sun is warming as my father's smile; the wind as caressing as my mother brushing my hair.

Richard Louv, in his book, *Last Child in The Woods: Saving Our Children From Nature Deficit Disorder*, shares my concerns about our children's disconnect from nature through the prevalence of television, air conditioning, computers, video games and our underlying parental fear of "the bogeyman." Louv is concerned that we are robbing our children of an essential connection and relationship to the earth. A connection that makes our children feel part of nature, not apart from it. A relationship that creates a sense of joy and wonder. A link that creates curiosity, meaning and context in all of our lives.

In our urban and suburban zoning, children are losing the creative interaction of playing in nature through tree house building. They are losing the opportunities for creek and wood exploration, and being alone; experiences that create confidence, self-reliance and a powerful sense of place. Many schools are shortening or eliminating recess and outdoor time, allowing our children even less interaction with the outdoors.

Twenty minutes of being outside can make the difference between having a good day or a bad day. Connecting to the earth can make the difference between having a joyful life or feeling lost and adrift.

Let's be creative to find ways to maximize our children's outdoor experiences. Let's give them the names of as many plants and animals as possible. Let's allow them to get dirty and mess up our yards, our parks and our playgrounds a bit with gardening and building exploration. Let's permit them to stay up to see Orion move over the horizon and command the myths of the sky. Let's teach them to pay attention to the minutiae of life—the clouds, the wind, the sounds of leaves, the flight of birds.

As Richard Louv writes, "Passion does not arrive on videotape or on a CD; passion is personal. Passion is lifted from the earth itself by the muddy hands of the young; it travels along grass-stained sleeves to the heart."

The Spiritual Role of Family

It's uncomfortable to consider. Some of us would rather not consider it at all.

To our children, we are their first experience of the divine, the all powerful, the all-knowing, with a human face. We fix ZuZu's petals. We are our children's miracle makers.

Our ability to create can be a double-edged sword by yielding the power to destroy or obstruct our children's development.

Our children come to us as spiritual embryos, beings working to build themselves. From birth, children have an inner life. Human development is a lengthy and internal process—an enigma that creates undeterminable results.

The problem with human development is the fact that the child has a spiritual life, even when he or she cannot express it. Because of the arduousness of this development, growth occurs over a long period of time. A child usually learns to walk by eighteen months of age. The effort the child uses to learn to walk is small compared to the internal work of the spirit.

A spirit is born, hidden in a small body, who little by little learns to exert his or her will in the world. The largest obstacle and the greatest help in the child's new world is the adult who has enormous power.

Like the physical body, the spiritual embryo must be protected in an environment filled with the richness of love and regard for the psychic development of the child.

As the adults, we have three principles that we should follow to protect the spirit of the child:

1. Respect all reasonable forms of activity in which the child engages and try to understand those activities.

2. We must support as much as possible the child's desires for activity. This doesn't mean that we wait on the child hand and foot, but we encourage activity in order to draw out the child's singular and independent spirit.

3. We must be careful in our relationships with children because they are quite sensitive, more than we know, to external influences.

I'm reminded of the movie, E.T., where three children discover an extra-terrestrial. The children are careful to help E.T. meet his needs and protect him from the adults who would capture, examine, and over-analyze him to death.

Let us observe children's activities and realize that these activities are the manifestations of the spirit within. Our children's activities are clues to their inner workings of spirit. Our children need our help to create an environment in which their spiritual embryos can grow stronger and healthier day by day.

As we observe our children, let us realize that tears, screams, misbehavior, shyness, disobedience, lying, egoism, and destructiveness are defense mechanisms of the child against us and are used as an attempt to gain our help to remove an obstruction to growth.

Children come to us very much as extra-terrestrials. We need to remember that children are new souls to this planet.

Let us strive to be sensitive to our children's needs, both physical and spiritual.

Turning Fear Into Love

Fear is a powerful motivator and behavior modifier. Fear, though, does not promote growth. Fear doesn't promote kindness, caring or compassion in ourselves. Fear doesn't open our hearts to new experiences. Fear doesn't connect us to other people.

What is the opposite of fear?

Love.

The opposite of love is not hate, but fear. Hate refers to a strong preference. When we dislike something we say, "I hate broccoli." When we prefer something above all else, we say we love it. "I love butter pecan ice cream. I hate bumble gum ice cream." In other instances when we use the word hate, we should perhaps substitute the word fear. "I fear war."

The word love is used in two basic ways—to express preference and to express an ability to be open and accepting of a person, place, thing or situation.

With love we accept the entire experience of a relationship. A horse-loving friend embraces the ups and downs of owning a horse. Danielle rides everyday. She sings "What A Beautiful Morning" mucking the stall. Horse smells invigorate her. Money spent on her mare, Misty, is never wasted. Two hours spent brushing Misty fly. With her horse, Danielle takes the good with the bad, and doesn't worry about getting kicked or thrown. Danielle understands the nature of horses, is cautious and aware, but not fearful.

Danielle's sister, Martha, on the other hand, appreciates her sister's horse, but Martha doesn't care to be involved in any aspect of being with a horse. Martha is not open to the horse experience. She considers horses to be dirty and smelly, and a drain on finances and time. Because a horse kicked a friend, Martha fears being hospitalized by a horse.

Danielle wanted to share her love of horses with Martha, and to help Martha lose her fear. Danielle convinced Martha to help groom Misty. At first Martha was hesitant about touching Misty, but after a few visits, Martha was bringing carrots and braiding Misty's mane. As Martha's experience and knowledge increased, her fearfulness diminished, and she began to seek out new experiences with Misty and Danielle. Martha found that facing her fears helped her feel more courageous in other aspects of her life. Martha attributed her connection to Misty as the impetus for a balloon ride and deciding to go to grad school.

Fear causes us to retreat from life. As Franklin D. Roosevelt said in his first inaugural address:

> ...let me assert my firm belief that the only thing we have to fear is fear itself—nameless, unreasoning, unjustified terror which paralyzes needed efforts to convert retreat into advance.

Being open to the experiences a relationship has to offer, having realistic expectations by seeing the positive with the negative of the situation, and serving the needs of others are expressions of love.

In St. Paul's famous letter to the Corinthians, he tells us,

> Love is patient, love is kind and is not jealous; love does not brag and is not arrogant, does not act unbecomingly; it does not seek its own, is not provoked, does not take into account a wrong suffered, does not rejoice in unrighteousness, but rejoices with the truth; bears all things, believes all things, hopes all things, endures all things. Love never fails...

Substitute *fear* for love and Paul's passage might read like this:

Fear is impatient, fear is not kind and is jealous; fear brags and is arrogant, and acts unbecomingly. It seeks its own, is easily provoked, takes into account a wrong suffered, does not rejoice in righteousness, but mocks the truth; fear destroys all things, believes in nothing, hopes for nothing, endures nothing. Fear always fails...

When we are afraid, let us gain the necessary knowledge and experience in order to transform fear into love. It is in facing our fears that we look into the eyes of love.

Let us show our children how to turn away from fear and towards love, knowing that love never fails. That would be a perfect Valentine.

The Metamorphosis of Childhood

Most ten-year-olds can tell you the stages of development for a butterfly or a frog. A butterfly begins as an egg, becoming a larva, a caterpillar, then a chrysalis emerging into a butterfly. A frog starts as an egg, hatching into a tadpole, turning into a polliwog, at last transforming into an adult frog. At each stage of change the frog and butterfly have differing needs for nourishment and environment.

As human beings, we also go through distinct changes, perhaps not with the physical drama of a butterfly or frog, but with identifiable changes in behavior with indicated physical and psychological needs. Too many times children are treated as though they are miniature adults. The human being, though, does not fully reach adulthood until around the age of twenty-four years.

In the infant who cannot feed him or herself, it is easy for us to observe the swift changes of the first two years of life. By the age of three years, a child learns to crawl, walk, talk, and eat table food, along with a multitude of self-care skills that help the child become more independent from caregivers.

Unfortunately for many of our children, this early independence leads adults to think that children three years and older are tiny grown-ups. Many of us are more aware of the requirements of cocoons and polliwogs than children's needs between the ages of three to six years.

The three to six-year-old is in a period of unconscious learning, absorbing information about his or her time and place from every aspect of the immediate environment. The child is unaware of learning and chooses to place his or her attention on activities that are repeated frequently. The child watches, listens, copies others and learns. This style of learning creates the following distinct needs for the young child:

- A need for an environment rich in language and experiences as vocabulary and story-telling capabilities are developed.
- A need to use his or her hands to connect the body and the brain to the realities of life.
- A need to create an emotional foundation built on the love, trust and respect of surrounding adults.
- A need to repeat activities in order to develop self-mastery and independence.
- A need for direct guidance on how to interact with people—within the family and the larger social network of school, church and other activities.
- A need for opportunities to refine the five senses of hearing, seeing, tasting, smelling and touching and to connect precise language to those experiences.
- A need for truthful and accurate information as the young child doesn't have a wealth of

experiences to discern between fact and fiction, fantasy and reality.

- A need for movement as the brain requires the body's motions for optimum neural development.
- A need for opportunities to exercise his or her will by having freedom within limits that enlarge as skills grow.

During this period of building foundational skills, the child is laying the groundwork for the adult he or she will become. The child is father to the man.

As the first tooth is lost and adult teeth emerge around the ages of six or seven years, the child begins a different phase of development. At this age, we notice that the baby face look of the younger child is replaced by a taller thinner appearance. The older child wants opportunities to go out into the world and step outside the familiar circle of family, school and church; desires novel experiences; is concerned with friends and working in a group instead of focusing on personal skills; wants to know why and problem solve; is concerned with learning about right and wrong; and desires an idea of the big picture of the universe.

Observe the differences between a four-year-old and a seven-year-old and you should see creatures as different as a larva to a caterpillar, or a tadpole to a polliwog.

We'd make sure a caterpillar had the right leaves to eat, and a polliwog had a pond. Let's use our influence as adults to create a world where our children have the opportunities to grow and change in the time specific ways children need.

Learning from Bumps and Bruises

As I visit with preschool administrators around the country a common theme emerges: the dynamics of smaller families are affecting children's abilities to learn how to endure the bumps and bruises of everyday life.

Many school principals and teachers hear from upset parents the first few days and weeks of school because children go home and complain about preschool. Used to being the center of attention of adults who listen and take care of their every request, these children are frustrated by the interpersonal demands of a preschool classroom.

"I told my friend I wanted to use the crayons and she didn't listen."

"I hurt my knee on the playground and I didn't get a Shrek bandage."

"I didn't eat snack because they didn't have my favorite cookies."

"I didn't get a turn on the swing."

Teachers report that parents are increasingly reluctant to let children endure any discomfort. These parents are more likely to remove their children from preschool than in previous years. Teachers say that parents in the quest to raise a perfect child have forgotten that important, yet basic, lessons are learned the hard way. We break a treasured toy. Friends don't listen to us. Friends won't play the game we want to play. We skin our knees on the playground. Lunch isn't our favorite hamburger with fries. Somehow in these interactions we learn important coping skills.

At the moment of our discomfort most of us are usually not happy campers. In retrospect, though, we may see a pattern of rough moments that have polished our character into a gemstone. The hurts endured—a friend sitting with someone else, of being hungry and not liking the foods offered—are growth experiences. These situations help us become resilient.

I'm reminded of six-year-old Caiti who visited my home. We found only one thing in the kitchen that Caiti could eat on her wheat free diet. Crunchy peanut butter. I knew that Caiti preferred smooth.

"I'm sorry Caiti, but I only have crunchy."

"That's fine, Caiti said. "I'll deal with it."

Caiti exhibits the kind of flexibility that comes with getting a few bumps and bruises and knowing that somehow it's all going to be okay. Not everything is going to go your way in life, and we do our children a disservice when we try to protect them from every disappointment or discomfort.

"Our greatest glory is not in never failing, but in rising up every time we fail," wrote Ralph Waldo Emerson.

There will be ups and downs in our children's lives. It is the small irritations that smooth and polish character as our children learn to take the good with the bad, and to get up every time circumstances knock them for a loop.

Remember that any unnecessary help is a hindrance to a child's development. Everyday jostlings teach our children to have the flexibility and strength to keep moving forward in order to enjoy and appreciate the experience of being alive.

Experiencing the Moment

My friend, Anita, recently wrote me about her adventures of accompanying her five-year-old granddaughter and daughter-in-law to private school enrollment interviews and classroom visits.

Eliana came out of one school interview jumping and twirling around and exclaimed, "That was so much fun!"

A week later at another interview session Eliana was the last to leave the classroom. Her grandmother described Eliana as quiet and contained. After they were in the car, Eliana's mother asked Eliana about the difference in her reaction to the two different school sessions.

Eliana told her mother and grandmother, "At this school I can put my happiness and joy inside the class."

"Which school do you like better?" Eliana's mom asked.

"I like this school because here I can just be myself. This was better."

Reading Anita's story made me think. How many times do we misinterpret our children's excitement as happiness, when in fact it might be exactly the opposite?

"Excitement may not be as satisfying as being where you can feel yourself in the right place of learning," Anita wrote.

Eliana knew. If we are in the right place at the right time, we experience a deep and quiet contentment, an intense satisfaction.

When we are in a place that doesn't engage our inner being, we may feel that we are only being entertained. The excitement generated from being thrilled or amused may keep us from being ourselves, from thinking our own thoughts, from making our own decisions.

We may all be able to do something to excite and entertain a child and make them squeal with delight.

It takes a special person to create a place where, as Eliana says, "I can put my happiness and joy inside."

Creating the right place at the right time requires knowledge of the needs of the people who will be using the space. It requires careful observation of the activities that hold significance. It requires preparing a place for people to engage in these meaningful activities.

Our fundamental needs can be considered as material and spiritual. Material needs include food, clothing, shelter and protection. Spiritual needs include appreciation of beauty and the arts, and communing with a higher power. Humans have inherent tendencies to be involved in activities, to have a sense of belonging, to feel a sense of growth, to explore, to orient themselves to new circumstances, to create order, to communicate needs and emotions, to use their imaginations, to repeat activities and to strive for perfection. There are many requirements for a place where we can put our joy.

To develop the right space we need to observe the activities of people being served. Perhaps because I love to cook and eat, I think of restaurants when considering environments. Savvy restaurant owners carefully watch the needs and activities of the people they serve. Well-run restaurants take careful note of what dishes their customers enjoy, what music they prefer to listen to, what decorations they appreciate. Fast food restaurants design environments for customers who want to meet the basic need of hunger quickly and inexpensively. Five stars restaurants cater to the need for nourishment, but may focus more attention on the esthetic needs and tendencies of their customers.

Successful restaurateurs plan spaces based on their observations of customer needs and behaviors. Designers consider table placement, colors, flowers, music, lighting, menus, table service and more to meet customers' material and spiritual needs, along with people's tendencies towards activity, communication, belonging, use of imagination, etc.

The teacher in a vibrant classroom considers the requirements of students in much the same manner as a restaurant manager with his customers—by understanding the fundamental needs of children, by observing children's activities, and by preparing an environment that supports those needs and actions.

That's how we can create the right space at the right time, a place for our children to put their joy and happiness inside. A place to experience the moments of their lives.

You Can't Say You Can't Play

Exclusion begins early in life, and can be observed even in preschool settings. In days a class divides up into three main groups—leaders who say who gets to play in their games, the children excluded from the games, and the children in the middle who live in fear of being rejected.

For the kindergartner who finds social skills a challenge, the exclusion of the playground becomes a self-fulfilling prophecy: a child isn't included in a game because he plays too rough, wears different clothes, or has a speech impediment. The list of deficiencies is long. Once the "in" group rejects this child the exclusion isolates the outcast child from the other children in all three groups.

The child is in quarantine from the group leaders, since it was the leaders saying, "you can't play" that created the exclusion in the first place. The rejected child is segregated from the other rejected children who are afraid of being further ostracized by the leaders. The third group forms with the children in the middle who are disinclined to play with the excluded children in case the leaders also tell them that they can't play.

Preschoolers create a caste system and change can be an impossible task.

Vivian Gussin Paley, nearing her 60th birthday and forty years of working with preschoolers and kindergartners, decided to test for herself whether this caste system she had observed for so many years, and at that point considered inevitable, could in fact be broken.

Paley begins by putting a sign on the wall—You Can't Say You Can't Play—(also the title of her book) and starts discussions with her kindergartners about her proposed rule. "Is it fair?" Paley asks. Paley knows she needs these five-year-olds to buy into the change.

Paley talks with her students to help the children figure out "who is sadder, the one who isn't allowed to play or the one who has to play with someone he or she doesn't want to play with?"

An outcast child, Clara, says it's sadder if you can't play.

Lisa, an excluding leader, says, "The other one is the same sadder."

Angelo, a loner, helps Lisa and the rest of the class understand. "It has to be Clara, because she puts herself away in her cubby. And Lisa can still play every time."

Inspired by a bird that followed Paley on a morning run, Paley uses the adventures of Magpie to weave a serial story, a journey of loneliness and exclusion with a cast of princes, princesses and animals that parallels events in the classroom.

Paley talks to the older grades about the rule. Older children think it is a good idea, but tell Paley that they are perhaps too old for the rule to be effective, because they are already too hurt to trust others.

When Paley moves to institute the rule in her classroom after weeks of discussing the implications of the rule and the unfolding of the Magpie story, Paley is amazed at how quickly the culture changes in her room, from exclusion to inclusion.

With her rule Paley uncovers a fundamental truth: "We must be told, when we are young, what rules to live by. The grownups must tell children early in life so that that myth and morality proclaim the same message while the children are still listening."

Paley begins her book with Leviticus 19:34:

The stranger that sojourneth with you shall be unto you as the home born among you, and thou shalt love him as thyself; for you were strangers in the land of Egypt.

Each of us is born a stranger into a strange land. If I could be Queen For A Day, I'd ask parents and teachers around the world to read Paley's *You Can't Say You Can't Play.*

As Paley tells us, "each time a cause for sadness is removed for even one child...we all rise in stature..."

We all could stand a little taller.

Relight the Candle

Five-year-old Tommy walked over to his mother, Judy. "Write my name for me, Mommy."

"Tommy, you know how to write your name."

"But I don't 'member," he said.

Tommy's mother, Judy, phoned me, near tears, about this conversation. Judy's concern was that Tommy had forgotten something as seemingly simple as the three letters in Tom.

"What do you think? Should I call my pediatrician? Do you think Tom has brain damage from falling off his bicycle two weeks ago? Should we get an MRI? A CAT scan?"

"Judy," I said, "I don't think there is probably anything serious going on. I think what you are seeing is a normal part of learning. The candle blew out. Tommy just needs to review and relearn how to write his name. It's very normal for children to forget things we think they have learned."

As learning occurs we take in information though our senses and retrieve this information through the memory process. The first time we encounter information doesn't mean we'll remember or retain it. How many repetitions does it take to learn a new phone number?

(Safety note: Cell phones seem to make learning phone numbers obsolete. Every five-year-old should know by heart his or her address and key phone numbers—home, parent's work, grandparents, etc.)

Some of us can hear a number or look at it once and have it in firmly in memory. For others it may take over a hundred repetitions. Learning theory suggests that most learning requires two hundred or more repetitions.

The process of retrieving facts from memory after they have been learned is another obstacle to a person's performance.

For example, I used to know my chocolate chip cookie recipe without hesitation since I made them a couple of times a week. (Oops! My secret is out.) In the past three or four years, though, I've made a batch only once. As I pulled out the mixing bowl my mind went black. Use it or lose it they say. How true it is for youngsters…and us older youngsters.

The more ways we can use information the better able we are to quickly access that information. When we can involve our hands in the memory and retrieval process, long-term learning is helped.

Repetition is a vital key to learning. The young child before the age of six enjoys doing the same activity over and over. How many times can a three-year old watch a favorite video? No number that large? Repetition is how the child creates memory and retrieval skills. Sameness creates a sense of order in the child's mind.

Children over the age of six are more adult like in their learning and demand variety in the presentation of information being acquired. How many times do adults like to watch a movie?

Skill building weaves in and out of our memories, flickering at the flame of knowledge. At times due to factors in brain development not entirely understood, this flame grows faint or is extinguished. At these times we need to patiently present previously learned information to the child—perhaps dozens of times. At some point, the information will be firmly set in the child's mind and will be remembered and easily retrieved.

The thousands of skills your child is acquiring take hundreds of repetitions each to become well established in the mind. Knowledge and skills will come and go as these hundreds of thousands of repetitions occur. Be patient and kind, and relight the candle. Make sure you have a big box of matches.

The Seeds of Passion

The purpose of education, I believe, is to help a child find his or her passion in life.

Passion comes from the heart and not the intellect. It's not about how much you know. It's about how much you care. Enthusiasm is a synonym for passion with one of the definitions for passion being "boundless enthusiasm."

Education, from the Latin, *educare*, means to draw or lead out. Education might be considered the process in which we help a child's personality unfold, much like a flower forming from a bud.

Optimism resides in flowering passion, as does excitement, emotional attachment and sense of purpose.

With passion we realize we have options, choices and opportunities. With this recognition enthusiasm follows.

Aristotle said, "Where talents and the needs of the world intersect, therein lies your vocation." Today we might say: where your passion and the needs of the world intersect, therein lies your life's calling.

As we help our children uncover their talents and gifts, while helping them realize they each have a special role and purpose in the world, passion will be revealed.

To uncover talents, one must "know thyself" by looking and listening to messages from the heart. The glimmerings of talent are shown through a person's interests and connection to people and objects in his or her environment. Children reveal their interests and the seeds of passion, but often there is no one looking, ready to draw out and lead that interest into passion.

Four-year-old boy Simon spent his three-hour preschool session aimlessly walking around the lab school classroom, day after day, week after week. No activity seemed to hold his interest. The lab school trainer asked a student teacher to observe Simon to see if the student could discern any type of interest Simon might have.

After a couple of days, as Simon walked round and round the classroom, the student noticed that Simon stopped during each rotation and touched the top of a book in the reading corner.

Looking at the book, the student observer noticed a miniature of a flag on the cover.

The following day, the student observed Simon touch the picture of the flag. The student reported this hint of interest to the trainer.

"Do you like flags?" the trainer went to the boy and asked.

"Yes," Simon said.

"Would you like to learn to embroider a flag?"

The trainer showed Simon how to place stitches on a cloth drawing.

The next morning Simon entered the classroom, going right to work on sewing his flag. As morning dismissal time arrived, Simon requested to stay and work in the afternoon.

"Can you call my mommy and ask if I can stay. But please don't tell her about the flag. I want to give it to her as a birthday present tomorrow."

The next afternoon, a glowing four-year-old Simon left his classroom clasping a decorated paper bag. For his mother.

From that day forward, Simon's interests in varying activities and his enthusiasm for interacting in the classroom grew. Connecting Simon's love for his mother and his interest in flags, helped his personality unfold, and his passion appear.

Watch for glimmerings of interest. Handle with care. Our children's seeds of passion reside there.

Need + Talent + Passion = Power

In his book, *The Eighth Habit*, Stephen Covey writes, "When you can give yourself to work that brings together a need, your talents and your passion, power will be unlocked."

The bluntness of that statement knocks the breath out of me, because isn't that what every one of us is looking for?

We spend our youth trying to discover our talents and our passion in life. If we are lucky enough to find and understand our gifts and enthusiasm, our next challenge is to find people who need our talents and passion. At the moment the third cherry, other's needs, comes round on the slot machine of life, we hit the jackpot.

At that juncture, if we will act with courage to fill the need we see, we gain the power to create.

When passion, talent and need come together, we have motivation and energy and the desire to learn skills that match our talent and passion.

Our job as parents and teachers is to help our children uncover their talents and passion. When our children realize the world's needs, large or small, we can be confident that they will respond with ability.

Don't we enjoy doing business with the bookstore clerk who loves literature, the coffee shop owner who is passionate about roasting beans, and the bike shop where designing your perfect bike is tantamount? Need, talent, passion have created power.

Seven-year-old Tyrone had difficulty reading and doing math, but Tyrone arrived at school everyday with a smile on his face, ready to be with his friends and to learn something new.

Tyrone knew everybody's lunchbox, coat, gloves, mittens, scarves, notebooks, dogs' names, date of birth, you name it. But 7 + 2? Forget about it.

Tyrone's classroom had an outdoor fishpond that required regular upkeep. The pond's pH needed to be tested, leaves removed, lilies fertilized, fish fed, and breathing holes chopped into the ice, among other pond keeping chores. Tyrone volunteered to care for the pond on weekends and vacations. If Tyrone was ill, he asked for a classmate to check on "his" fish.

Tyrone was passionate about the fish and wanted to make sure they had everything they needed to live. Though Tyrone struggled to read, he pored over articles on how to take care of the fish and test the hydrogen levels in the pond. Tyrone charted the chemical readings with decimal numbers even though he could barely add two plus two. Visitors to the classroom were offered a tour of the fishpond, with Tyrone proudly telling about the life cycle of fish and the eco-dynamics (his word) of a small pond.

Tyrone's talent and passion for caring about living things, when added to the needs of the pond, unleashed a power in him to learn what some might have thought impossible for a seven-year-old with learning challenges.

Let's help our children find their passion and develop their talents. The world needs their gifts and enthusiasm.

A Thank You Walk

"I'm worried that my four and six-year-old will be spoiled. They have such a great life—plenty of love, food, toys, and money. I want them to be thankful for what they have," Melinda said.

Melinda understood that helping her children cultivate an attitude of gratitude was important to her children's present and future happiness. Too many parenting magazines today feature advertisements with well-dressed children who appear bored and pouty, lacking excitement and engagement with life. Melinda didn't want that kind of person living in her house.

Expressing thanks and gratitude is a trait that leads to happiness, and we need to help our children learn how to give thanks. I mentioned to Melinda that I'd come across an idea that I hadn't personally used but sounded intriguing, a thank you walk.

The suggestion for the walk was to take your children out and express thanks for items you come along in your journey. The adult models gratefulness and challenges the children to look at the world with eyes of thankfulness.

I thought this game could be particularly poignant on those grumpy days when appreciation has flown out the window. Get out on a walk and find it!

Melinda reported a few weeks later that her family had taken a Sunday afternoon thank you walk. After the walk they came back home and drew pictures and recapped their thanks on a list that went on the refrigerator. Melinda shared the list with me.

We're thankful for…

Our raincoats

Our rain boots

The sidewalk

That our neighbor has pretty flowers in her yard

That trees have leaves we can jump in

That apples grow on trees

That we can climb in trees in our backyard

That we have arms and legs to climb

That we have a cool fort in our backyard

That we have a dog

That we can walk to the park

That we can meet grandma and grandpa at the park

That grandma makes pies and always has ice cream

That grandpa bought me a building kit

That I have a shelf in my room for my building kits

Worms

Ladybugs

Bees

Hummingbirds

Robins

Clouds

The sun

Rainbows

My brother

My mom and dad

Melinda was pleased how her boys joined in with enthusiasm in finding things to be thankful for. An attitude of gratitude is worth cultivating. All you have to do is look around.

Effective Skill Building

Research shows that learning new skills in the most efficient manner requires self-discipline and practice. That seems like commonsense to most of us. Science is confirming that, yes, to get better you've got to make yourself sit at the piano and play those tunes and do those finger exercises. Every day.

Effective learning or skill building occurs when we can maximize these factors:

1. We have the ability to focus our attention on the task at hand.

2. We have control over the choice of the task.

3. The task if meaningful to us and we understand how to do it.

4. We have adequate time to practice the task, which research shows to be 60 to 90 minutes per day.

5. We control feedback, which is accurate and timely.

6. We have the opportunity to repeat the task daily or many times per week.

7. We have overnight rest between practice sessions.

Ability to focus. Learning to focus can be difficult with the distractions of everyday life. There may always be something more interesting than what someone else wants us to learn, which makes the next point critical.

Choice of the task. When we feel that we have control over what tasks we do and when we do them, we tend to learn more quickly. If we know we do better with math early in the morning when we are fresh, we'll learn more quickly if we can make the choice to do math in the morning.

Meaningful tasks. Haven't we all taken a class and wondered, "When will I ever need to know this stuff?" We learn more quickly when tasks connect to our everyday life and we understand how to do the task. Do you remember the first time you cracked an egg? Having a clear vision of how to perform the task helped. Meaningful? Doing it right meant the difference between scrambled and sunny side up, or in the dish versus on the floor.

Adequate time. Research shows that children will stay on a learning task for 60 to 90 minutes if the task is meaningful, if the individual child has choice about the task, and if the child is interested in the task. When these conditions are present for learning and the meaningful, chosen, and interesting task is interrupted because of time constraints, learning goes down the tubes and self-motivation takes a nosedive.

Learner controlled feedback. We learn best when we get accurate feedback about our progress when we desire it. Self-correcting materials are ideal learning aids. Having the correct answers available immediately aids learning. Ever try to work a thousand piece puzzle without looking at the picture? It's probably ten times easier to put it together with a picture because you get the timely and accurate feedback needed to figure out the puzzle.

Daily repetition. People who excel in an area know that they need to be involved in meaningful tasks everyday to grow and maintain skills and knowledge. We need to make sure we allow the time every day to take on the challenge of learning.

Overnight rest. As many college graduates will confess, you can't cram a semester's worth of learning into a one-day event. Study an hour a day for twelve days and you'll learn more Anatomy 304 than twelve hours in one day. Daily repetition and overnight rest is one reason schools and businesses run on a five-day a week schedule. It helps people learn and grow.

Understand and use these seven points to aid effective learning in your children's and your personal development.

SPIRES
Seeing the Big Picture

---

pires and inspiration have the same root word, *spire,* from the Latin meaning to breathe in. The ancient Greeks and Romans thought that when humans had an inspiration it was due to the fact that they had inhaled the breathe of the gods.

When we look up we naturally take an inward breathe. Brain researchers know that we can change our perception and mood to be more positive by the simple act of moving our eyes upward.

Looking up, taking in the positive, setting high goals and seeing the big picture are symbolized by the spires of our cathedrals.

We need to build spires and contemplate them. In our upward gazing our thought processes transform.

Looking up to see the big picture, inspiration has a chance to claim us, as we partake the breathe of the gods.

Santa Claus: Making the Invisible Visible

"I've never gotten a present from Santa Claus," said Iliana, my 12-year-old seatmate on an east coast flight. "My parents thought I should only be given verifiable facts. They told me there is no veracity in Santa Claus."

"It's too bad that no one ever told your parents about the Secret of Santa Claus. When you know the Secret, you believe in Santa Claus all your life, even if you can't verify facts," I said.

"You believe in Santa Claus? What secret?"

"It's simple, but..."

"Please, tell me," Iliana said.

"We're flying on a plane right now. Who built this plane? Who designed it? Who got it ready to fly? Who trained our pilots? We know that someone had to do it, and with some research we could find those people. We won't though. We'll never meet those people. I'll call them invisible workers since they work to give us something we couldn't do alone."

I took a sip of coffee. "There are thousands of invisible workers for almost everything we use. I have no idea who planted the beans for this cup of coffee, or who picked them, roasted them and packaged them. I can only thank our flight attendant, the last person in this invisible line of people."

"I have faith," I continued, "that when I wish to fly on an airplane, or have a cup of coffee, these unknown people will have done their jobs, and my desires will come true. I don't have to grow my own coffee beans, build my own airplane, because of all these wonderful people."

"So you're saying that Santa Claus is an invisible worker?" said Iliana.

"I see Santa Claus being all these people in the world, who strive to serve humankind, to make life more enjoyable, more comfortable, more magical. I will never see these people who do so many things for me, but they are most assuredly real. When I understood this, and I was older than twelve, I wanted to be that helpful kind of person. In the first stage of believing in Santa Claus, when we're little, we're on the receiving end. When we live the secret, we are on the giving side, which is fun. Being like Santa, which is doing our jobs with cheerful intention to help others, makes amazing things happen, such as flying at 30,000 feet at 500 miles an hour, while sipping coffee, and talking to you about Santa Claus."

"I get it. Once you know how Santa works you become Santa Claus. You do your regular stuff with love in your heart, and try to help others not expecting anything in return. Santa is people helping people. I'm pretty sure nobody told my parents that." Iliana said. "I think I'm going to have some fun being an invisible worker."

I was hoping I could show Iliana that Santa is that invisible force of faith, charity, believing and doing that cannot be easily explained. For the young child, one way we can help them see and experience this force is in Santa's work. As the young child enters a developmental stage of reasoning, around age six, and begins to wonder about Santa, we need to give them opportunities to work and contribute to something bigger than themselves. We need to show them how to choose to be part of the magical power of giving, service and surprise.

As we walked off the plane, Iliana said, "I'm so excited about Santa Claus. I've already got some great ideas. I think this feeling is what the saying 'it is more blessed to give than to receive' means. Boy, are my parents and a few other people going to be surprised."

Iliana spied her grandparents and started singing "Here Comes Santa Claus." They laughed and said, "What are you so happy about?"

As I walked away, Iliana waved and winked at me, then answered, "It's a secret."

Every Day a Little Play

Tempers were short. Especially mine. The girls had been sick and cranky. It had rained for several days. We were moving to a new town. My husband had been gone for ten days. Real estate showings interrupted nap and dinner times. There were boxes to pack. Everything seemed so serious.

A friend from our Active Parenting class called to invite the girls and me to lunch. "I don't know if you want us, Tammy. No one in this house has a sense of humor right now."

"Remember from class? Every day a little play. Are you remembering to have fun?"

What a friend to remind me of the important stuff. In the thousands of tasks I thought I had to do, I wasn't doing anything fun with the girls. So, off we went to make cookies. We sang and acted silly. In a matter of thirty minutes, all the crabs left the house. Cooperation and cheerfulness were restored by just a little play. How simple it can be, and so hard to remember.

Once a situation or relationship begins a downward spin, it seems impossible to turn it around. We wait for the dreaded "crash and burn" of tempers flaring. I've learned that the advice in "everyday a little play" can create positive relationships with children, and help anger and tension melt away. Play needn't be as complicated or messy as baking cookies. Five minutes of focused fun can turn a situation around.

The boys in my kindergarten class were being uncooperative about their lessons. Tasks were not being completed, or silly antics kept pulling the concentrated students off focus. I asked one of my students why he didn't want to work on a math lesson. Kelly looked up with big blues eyes and said, "All we do is work, work, work. When can we have some fun?"

Oops. Out of the mouth of babes. I had forgotten (again) about a little play. "What would be fun, Kelly?"

"If you'd play soccer with us."

Out we went for fifteen minutes of soccer. It was Kelly who stopped the action and said, "I'm ready to do some math work."

I resolved then and there to have some fun everyday with my students, and make sure I laughed with them everyday. We had treasure hunts, played catch, sang songs, popped corn, played word games, and did parachute activities. When I made sure to have some silly fun and not be so serious about all the work we needed to do, I found my kindergartners becoming harder workers and more cooperative.

Take a little trip down memory lane. What was a fun activity that you and one of your parents shared? Close your eyes and visualize the fun experience. How did you feel about your parent at that moment? How did you feel about yourself?

Take at least five minutes a day to do something fun with each of your children. After each experience, jot down on the calendar what you did and how it went. This will help you see what is working and what is not. Using the calendar may also help you make a habit of "everyday a little play." Remembering to play can save the day.

1969...1969...1969...

It was a bathroom mirror moment—one of those seconds where you stand between two mirrors and see yourself patterned to infinity.

Mindy, our neighborhood babysitter, sorted pennies by date, with my daughters, then three and five years old. I walked in from the dentist office, minus two wisdom teeth. I'll admit I wasn't at the top of my game.

"Here is a 1969," Mindy said. "The year I was born."

"But you aren't old enough to be born in 1969," I said. "That means I could have babysat you."

Mindy, too polite to say "Duh!" smiled at me. "I really was born in 1969."

The mirrors in my mind swung into place, and I glimpsed a pattern. The children I babysat could be my children's babysitters. In these reflected images I saw that my daughters could be Mindy's children babysitters. And Mindy's children could baby-sit my grandchildren. And my grandchildren could...

I had to sit down. My head hurt. I never realized babysitting had so many complicated inter-connections.

Flash forward to 1996. "It's weird," my eighth-grade daughter said at dinner one night. "I found out today that four of my teachers are 27 years old. Weird. Four teachers born in 1969."

Once more a mirrored moment showed me another connection in the pattern. My daughter's babysitters were now their junior-high teachers. My daughters would soon be babysitting their children.

I saw links going backwards. I followed connections forward.

The children I babysat in 1969 were now my children's teachers. The 1969er's children would soon be in my classroom. The three-year-olds that were in my classroom might baby-sit my yet-to-be born grandchildren. And be their teachers. Yikes! Did I have some work to do.

At that moment, how I wished I had been a better babysitter. How I wished I'd coached my babysitters more. I hadn't realized they would be teaching my children for years to come. Had I taught my daughters enough so they could do their parts as babysitters, students, teachers, parents…etc.? Was I keeping my eye on my goals and purposes?

Our connections go deep and long. Each of us creates a pattern that travels forward and backwards. All of us have an important role to play in the lives of many people, whether we realize it or not. We each form a vital link in the continuing drama of human beings. Our jobs as student and teacher, parent and child, employer and employee, forge generations of relationships. As we move from role to role, we can only do the best we know how, and endeavor to do our parts with love and respect for those people in our lives.

Because our children are our grandchildren's parents. To infinity, and beyond.

Competition

The thirtyish-year-old father stood next to me on the playing field. We were watching his four-year old son's soccer team.

"I can't wait until Josh is old enough to play catch with me," he said.

"Josh is old enough to play catch with you now. Matter of fact, if you don't build that relationship now, when he's six or seven he'll choose his friends over you," I said. "When did your dad start throwing balls to you?"

April. We are in the middle of team sports—soccer, t-ball, softball, baseball, track. The trend nationwide seems to involve children as young as three or four in little-league clubs.

Why? Why do we feel that it's important for preschoolers to be involved in a team sport? Are team sports the right thing for our under-sixes?

Competition seems to mean, "to win" and that the most important result of competing is winning. The structure of team sports creates "winners" and "losers."

The word competition derives from the Latin, *com,* meaning with, and *petere,* to strive. To strive with others or to strive together. With competition, we become competent. Sports evolved from a desire or need to stay physically fit. There is nothing like signing up for a 10 K event with friends to help you roll out of bed for a 6 a.m. run.

In today's team sports for what are we striving together? What is our common goal? If it is only to accrue points and declare one group winners and another group losers, we fail our children.

Is our objective to learn to work together as a team? Is it to learn to take direction from a coach? Is it to learn to be gracious whether we win or lose, understanding that unless we have competitors, we cannot claim the title of winner?

Winning status is conferred on us by those who compete with us. Winning is bestowed by those who strive with us toward common goals. A true competitor understands this. If our common goal is to stay physically fit and active, we should realize that we work harder because of our competitors, win or lose, fast or slow, junior or varsity.

Our preschoolers are in a developmental period of self-mastery along with developing independence and concentration. Do our team sports for children under the age of six or seven aid this development? Most of my observations tell me no.

Many of our preschoolers are attending team practices and games when these children's needs could be better served by kicking and dribbling a soccer ball in their own backyard or in a park with parents or siblings. In a Costa Rican park I observed a lone three-year-old boy dribble and juggle a soccer ball for almost an hour. I lost concentration before he did.

Preschoolers need to be working on skills that promote self-mastery, independence and concentration. Around age six, children begin a developmental period where they enjoy and require group interaction and team building.

Let's give our preschoolers the time to develop close family relationships, master individual skills, develop physical and mental independence while acquiring strong focus doing age appropriate activities.

When our children, around age six or seven, are ready and ask to compete and work in a team, they will bring these foundational skills, strong relationships, self-reliance and concentration to their activities. Until then, let's allow preschoolers to be preschoolers.

Cloud Watching

Summer officially begins with the summer solstice on June 21. For kids, I believe in the words of the Nat King Cole song,

"Roll out those lazy, hazy, crazy days of summer." June, July and August should allow all of us time to luxuriate in some slow goofiness.

Summer is a period of tremendous physical growth for children. Many children can grow three or more inches in height during these three or four months, and add the pounds to go with the inches. It takes a lot of extra eating to put on a pound, as a pound of weight gain requires an additional 3500 calories.

During this period of physical growth the child needs a lot of fresh food, exercise and rest. During the summer it can appear that all kids want to do is sleep, play hard, eat, sleep and then do it all again.

We can observe physical growth easily enough and measure the increase with rulers and scales. Even though it may appear as if our children are doing nothing mentally productive during the summer, there is a lot of hidden intellectual growth occurring,

The time to be outdoors and chase bees, pick clover, dig lakes and make dams in the mud, have picnics, or lounge on a quilt and watch the clouds morph from giant bears to Abraham Lincoln, helps create mental connections that can only be made in an environment that is closer to boring than exciting.

As our children have the time to watch the clouds, a certain type of self-reliance emerges. The child is free to let his or her thoughts wander. With time to cloud watch instead of clock watch, our children have the opportunity to perhaps see their lives in a perspective not hemmed in by the demands of a daily routine.

Cloud watching is serious business and may not come intuitively to our children. We must model the ability to sit back and savor the passage of time.

Take a picnic blanket and head outdoors for a morning or afternoon of earnest cumulus, cirrus, stratus cloud viewing. (Be wary of chiggers, ticks and other unwanted visitors. Take sunscreen, hats, and sunglasses.) Lie down in a grassy spot and look up at the trees. Watch and then ask your children what kinds of things live in the trees. Can they see any animals in the tree? What else can they see? What sounds do they hear? What do they smell? Can they taste anything? What do they feel? What do the clouds make them think about?

Afterwards, either on your blanket or indoors, help your children write a sensory poem by asking the questions you asked outdoors. Invite them to illustrate their poems.

Here's a poem written by a five-year-old friend, after a session of thoughtful cloud watching. Perhaps these words will help you see some of what's growing inside a mind during those lazy, hazy, crazy days of summer.

Outside
I see the sky, the trees, a butterfly
I smell the grass
I hear the neighbor's lawnmower, the wind in the
trees
I feel the wind in my hair
I taste the air in my mouth
I kiss a cloud

I Dream of a World

—In honor of Martin Luther King Day 2008

I dream of a world where every person sees their own greatness and reaches for the vision they have for themselves.

I dream of a world where each parent gives power to their children's dreams and has faith in their children's journey.

I dream of a world where deep abiding love doesn't create the path for others, but lights a path.

I dream of a world where every child is born into a family that loves and nurtures him or her; a world where each person is respected and cherished.

I dream of a world where our lives are fueled by our imaginations and not by our histories.

I dream of a world where each child is given the keys to learning.

I dream of a world where children are given a vision of the universe.

I dream of a world where each of us can marvel at the big picture and understand how important each of us is to the whole of the universe.

I dream of a world where education helps children, and all of us, find our passion in life.

I dream of a world where each of us discovers our vocation in the place where our passion and the needs of the world intersect.

I dream of a world where supporting the development of caring, compassionate and cooperative adults is a priority.

I dream of a world where respect for human life creates a bridge of communication for all peoples.

I dream of a world where we learn to be healthy instead of waiting to be healed.

I dream of a world. I dream.

LABYRINTHS
Finding Personal Power

---

he floors of many cathedrals have designs that resemble mazes, and for years many people thought these designs served only as intricate patterns. The designs are in fact labyrinths.

In a maze, there are dead ends and confusion. A maze is a puzzle that you may or may not be able solve. In a labyrinth there is only one path, and that path leads you to the center and out again. As you walk the pattern of a labyrinth, a sense of calm overcomes you, problems that seem overwhelming begin to feel manageable, and agitation is replaced with meditation.

The labyrinth designs follow a predictable pattern much like inside a seashell. The labyrinth floor of the cathedral holds a key to a peaceful life. Walk purposefully and quietly to your center, listen to yourself, and think through your problems. The answers will follow.

In working with our children we need tools to help us listen to ourselves and others, to help us understand our roles as parents and teachers, and to work through the myriad of problems that are life.

We can follow a maze with its confusing purpose, or walk the labyrinth, where we are lead to the center of self-discovery and back out into the world to do our work.

Parenting and teaching require this internal search and understanding of ourselves before we can be of true help to children.

Five Steps to Problem Solving with Children

"Stop!" I heard six-year-old Alan tell a couple of three-year-old girls. "I think you've got a problem."

Lila and Susan, the three-year-olds, were tugging and grunting to see who would get possession of a puzzle. Alan continued, "I think you both want to do this puzzle by yourself. Do you want to work this out?"

Lila and Susan stopped, looked at Alan, and nodded in agreement. "You can either take turns or choose something else. What do you think is best?" Alan politely asked them.

I watched this classroom scene unfold as Susan decided to choose another puzzle and Lila promised to let Susan know when she was finished using the puzzle. No tears. No hitting. I witnessed peaceful problem solving with no adult intervention.

"No way!" you are probably thinking. "That's just not real." As a friend of mine said, "Alan sure doesn't sound like any six-year-old I know." It can be a typical scenario if we will show young children a simple five-step problem solving technique. By the time they are six, they will sound older than their years.

A basic ground rule in conflict resolution with children is that they must use their words to solve their problems. There is to be no hitting, biting, kicking, or name-calling; in short, no action intended to harm others may be used. The adult's initial role is to step the children through the process, acting as facilitator. Like Alan, at some point, the child will step into the facilitator's role. Let's look at this five-step problem solving method.

Step 1: Recognizing a Problem. In my example, six-year-old Alan saw two children struggling with a puzzle. So he said "Stop. I think you've got a problem." This statement helps those in conflict disengage and shift their focus. Sometimes just stopping will help us see our actions and change our behavior without any other intervention. If the behavior does continue, we need to make sure the children in conflict stop before we move to the next step in problem solving.

Step 2: Identifying the Problem. Alan at this point said, "I think you both want to use the puzzle at the same time." Susan or Lila might have said, "No, that's not the problem. She's putting the puzzle in the wrong place." As facilitators, we have to listen to make sure the problem is clearly stated and that everyone agrees to work on the problem before we move on to the next step.

Step 3: Brainstorming for Solutions. As adults, we'll see solutions to the problem before the children. State these and ask if they can think of any more suggestions. It's easy as an adult to want to quickly resolve a situation and force our solution. We're trying to teach the process, so give the children time to think of other solutions and evaluate all suggestions before moving on to the next step.

Step 4: Choosing the best solution. After the group agrees that they have looked at all the possible solutions, it will be time to pick the best one. Restate all the solutions and have them choose the best one. State the selected solution clearly, as in our example: Susan will choose another puzzle, and Lila promises to let Susan know when she is finished.

Step 5: Checking back to make sure it's working. This is the step that is easy to forget. It is important to check back with each person to make sure the solution is working. If not, call back the children and restart the problem solving process again.

The first few times as a facilitator with children, this process may seem very long and formal. I used to have a hand-made poster in my classroom to remind everyone of each step. Amazingly, using these five steps consistently, children realize the process works and will begin to problem solve on their own. Even after children are independently problem solving, we may have to step in every once in a while to get the process back on track.

Remember, we all forget once in a while! Be kind if you or the children do the steps less than perfectly. Children are resilient. One of my favorite parenting sayings is this: *It's hard to remember the objective is to drain the swamp, when you're up to your eyeballs in alligators.* Parenting is tough. We're all just trying to do the best we can.

Begin using this problem solving method with your three to six-year-olds to create a foundation for a lifetime of effective problem solving. What you might get in return is a teenager who, instead of slamming a door, comes to you saying, "Mom, Dad, I have a problem. Here are some possible solutions. Can you help me think of any more?' Stranger things have happened.

Consider using this problem-solving tool today, whatever your children's ages. Count to ten when the squabbling begins and use this five-step method to help your children learn to solve disputes.

Four Strategies to Deal with Problems

At a recent seminar, our speaker presented the idea that there are four basic strategies to deal with any problem: Ignore, Resolve, Manage, and Prevent. At first, the list appeared over-simplistic. Could ignoring a problem be an effective strategy? After some reflection, I recognized that ignoring a problem is a powerful strategy. Not every problem needs or deserves our attention. It's important to know when and how we should deal with a problem, and be able to prioritize our efforts.

The art of parenting includes choosing appropriate strategies and solutions for our problems. Life is problems and problem solving. Stating our problem in writing helps bring the problem clearly into focus.

There are five basic steps to problem solving.

1. Recognize that there is a problem.
2. State the problem.
3. Identify all possible solutions. (Using strategy is critical here.)
4. Choose a solution.
5. Implement the solution, and make sure it works.

Here is an example, not involving children, to help highlight these four strategies. You look out your front window and your neighbors have an old junk car parked in their yard. You could choose to ignore the situation, thinking it will be gone in a few days, since your neighbors have always kept a lovely yard.

To resolve it you might pick the phone and ask, "Bob, what year is that Chevy in your front yard?"

After trying to resolve it, using a management strategy might include not looking out your window, calling the neighborhood association, or paying for a tow truck, among others.

A prevention strategy could include creating a neighborhood rule against cars parked in the grass, developing good relationships with your neighbors, starting a beautification program, etc.

Dr. Phil McGraw, for his book, *Family First*, surveyed 1700 parents. The top three behavioral problems parents sited follows:

- Children not paying attention
- Children losing control or having tantrums
- Children talking back

To make our parenting job easier, it makes sense to strategize how to deal with or avoid these three problems. As the old saying goes, "An ounce of prevention is worth a pound of cure."

To prevent these three problems, create a family structure and relationship with your child so that the situations rarely or never occur.

- Teach your child to pay attention instead of having an inattention problem.
- Teach your child self-control and self-expression instead of allowing tantrums.
- Develop a relationship built on mutual respect to avoid the disrespect inherent in back talking.

Even if we do everything we can to prevent these problems, stuff will happen. There are too many things we cannot anticipate. When we have a difficulty we need to use all strategies to consider as many solutions as possible. With talking back, for example, ask these strategic questions:

How are we going to prevent our child from talking back?

If he or she does talk back, how are we going to manage that situation?

When we try to manage a situation, how are we going to resolve the issues that triggered the talking back?

How do we know when to ignore a disrespectful statement or when to escalate it to a resolution?

Use strategy to prevent, manage, resolve or ignore inevitable problems. That's life. Being strategic will help make the best of it.

The Rule of 150

The Rule of 150 states that the size of an effective social network is limited to 150 members. Social scientists theorize that 150 is the limit of the human ability to remember and respond to all the members in a group. The human mind seems unable to maintain a large number of distinct relationships.

As the number of members in a group approaches 150, certain dynamics begin to manifest themselves. Under 150 members, groups tend to be able to cooperate based on mutual trust, simple rules and easily understood management of resources. As the group approaches or exceeds 150 members, factions appear, and a leadership hierarchy emerges.

Military organizations, one of the oldest forms of working cohesive groups, know that people work best in groups limited to 150 or less, that is platoons and squadrons. A platoon contains 30 to 40 people, comprised of smaller working units. A squadron or company consists of 60 to 250 members comprised of two to six platoons. Companies or squadrons are considered minor units, in contrast to the major units of battalions and regiments, which may contain two to 24 squadrons or 300 to 3,000 soldiers.

A four-hundred-year-old religious group, the Hutterites, realized that their maximum size for a communal farm, or colony, was 150 people. As a colony approached 150 members, the Hutterites divided the colony in two separate groups, in order to avoid the splintering of the group into clans. Today the Hutterites have around 350 colonies with over 35,000 members.

As a group goes over 150, social scientists have noted that it is easier for freeloaders, cheaters and liars to establish themselves into the community, introducing a divisive element to the group.

What does the Rule of 150 mean for our families and our children?

As we work in groups, we need to be aware of the dynamics that naturally develop. A friend described how her workplace disintegrated as the group grew larger. "I remember," she said, "exactly the day, time and place that my job went from 'us' to 'them'. From that moment forward I watched the group splinter and our espirit de corps be lost forever."

In our schools, we need to encourage the creation of workings groups of less than 150 whenever possible. Communities tell of success in creating "schools within a school" programs or "pods," where less than 150 students and teachers interact in a long-term learning community. Families and school staff report a sense of high satisfaction when working in these smaller school organizations using multi-year tracts.

In our churches, we need to be aware of how growth affects the community. Pastors report political and leadership challenges as congregations approach 150 members. Fellowship groups of six to eight families or couples create vital social cohesion and group satisfaction in larger churches.

In our sports organizations, we need to use the Rule of 150 to keep our leagues small enough to avoid damaging trust, loyalty and the objectives of sportsmanship.

As a group reaches its effective limits, people start to fall through the cracks of the social network. Complicated hierarchies of leadership emerge. Communication and feedback diminish among members.

As we all know, there are still problems with groups that are under 150 members. In smaller organizations, though, perhaps our children and our families can develop effective relationships and communications, helping to ensure the happiness and success of each member.

Using Your Thinking Hats

Some women get rocks set into precious metals for anniversaries, birthdays or Christmas. I get books.

Over twenty years ago, my husband presented me with a jewel of a book for Christmas. I've used this gift to teach thinking skills to children and adults. The title? *Six Thinking Hats* by Edward De Bono.

De Bono, the creator of Lateral Thinking, uses the idea of six colored hats to represent the viewpoints needed for effective problem solving.

Pretending to wear colored hats permits us to role-play and remove our egos from the situation. Using the idea of the hats directs our attention to the critical aspects of a discussion. The hats create a convenient way to switch gears within a group, as the hats act as a tool to ask others to shift their thinking in specific ways.

Learning to use the six thinking hats helps us become more flexible and control moods. In the game of thinking, the hats give us a plan to map out the realities and possibilities of a situation.

White Hat Thinking is concerned with facts and figures and looks at the available data, past trends and holes in information.

Red Hat Thinking suggests emotions and takes in regard how we "feel" about the situation in regards to intuition, gut reactions and emotions.

Putting on *Black Hat Thinking* takes the "gloom and doom" view of the pessimist and asks why something might not work and what might go wrong.

The optimistic aspects and outcomes of the situation are considered in *Yellow Hat Thinking*, focusing on sunny and positive forecasts.

Green Hat Thinking finds fresh ideas and solutions using creativity and alternative methods, while reminding us that the grass always looks greener on the other side.

The Blue Hat Thinking governs the process of thinking. True blue and cool blue come to mind when we ask the right questions, define a problem and set the thinking tasks. In a group someone must wear the Blue Hat all the time, or put on the Blue Hat to redirect the process.

Let's take a problem using the hats to think through a situation. Twelve-year-old Tom has asked for a family meeting because he is missing $15.00 from his room.

Dad asks for everyone to put on Blue Hats to define the problem, which follows: Tom wants to figure out where the $15.00 went and how to keep his valuables safe.

Dad volunteers to wear the Blue Hat for this meeting. To gather pertinent facts, Dad asks for White Hat thinking. They discover that Tom's ten-year-old brother, Bobby, let a friend during a sleepover go into Tom's room. At that time, Bobby hadn't seen any money. Tom went to the mall on Friday. Did he take the money with him?

Red Hat Thinking is Dad's next request. Tom says he is mad that someone came into his room and that Bobby didn't watch his guest more closely. Mom said she felt that the money might be in the room somewhere, perhaps behind the dresser.

With her Black Hat on, Mom said perhaps we shouldn't have friends over. Dad said the worst is that we might not trust each other. Bobby said we might falsely accuse a friend of stealing.

Using Yellow Hat Thinking, the family thought they might find the money. The idea of being more careful with money was considered. They discussed off limit rules for friends, and locking bedroom doors.

With the Green Hat the family explored the possibilities of getting a safe, keeping all money in the bank and using ATM cards.

After the Six Hat session, Tom realized he needed to lock up his valuables and not leave cash in full view. Bobby realized he shouldn't allow his friends into Tom's room. Mom offered to take Tom and Bobby to the bank to set up accounts. Bobby offered to ask his friend if he had seen any money in Tom's room. Dad offered to help Tom look in his room for the money. By the way, the money was behind the dresser.

Using the Six Thinking Hats, Tom's family looked at a situation in a calm, organized way, exploring different viewpoints, while planning for the short and long term.

Why? Why? Why? Why? Why?

"For whatever reasons my eight-year-old, Eric, is critical of everything his younger siblings do. Eric tells his sister that her coloring stinks. He tells his brother that his handwriting is messy. Last night Eric burst into tears because the peas touched his mashed potatoes. Nothing seems to make him happy right now," Michael told me. "How can I fix it?"

"You can't fix it, Michael," I replied.

"What? There must be something I can do," Michael said.

"Of course, there's something you can do. But you need to involve Eric in the process. Don't try to fix Eric. Work with Eric to see what he is feeling and thinking."

I explained to Michael a probing technique taught to me by a philosopher friend called "The Five Whys." Dr. Carey maintained that if we asked why five times we could discover the root cause of a problem or a core value inherent in a situation.

Michael and I role-played for a few minutes with the five whys. I encouraged Michael to talk to Eric privately to get at the root of Eric's criticisms. Michael and Eric's conversation went something like this:

"Eric, why did you tell your sister that her coloring was messy?"

"Well, Dad, it is messy."

"Why do you think it is messy? Show me what you mean."

"Here, Dad. See, she colored way outside the lines. And there are scribbles everywhere."

"Why do you think she needs to color her pictures your way?"

"Because when she gets to third grade her teacher will make her do it over. And she will have to stay in at recess and do her work over."

"Why do you think it is not okay to do your work over, Eric?"

"If you do work over you miss recess and the teacher looks at you funny. And," Eric burst into tears, "your friends think you are a dork."

In only four why's Michael began to get a picture about the root cause of Eric's negative and critical behavior towards his siblings. Eric felt over whelmed by the standards set by his third-grade teacher.

In the spirit of "working with" Eric instead of trying to "fix" Eric, Michael asked, "Eric, how can I help you with your situation at school?"

Eric told his dad that he didn't need any help at school. "I can handle it, Dad," he said.

"Okay, then. But Eric, I want you to know that I am always here to help you when and if you need it.

"Sure, Dad."

"How can I help you be kinder to your brother and sister, since they're not in third-grade yet?"

"Gosh, Dad," Eric began to grin through his sniffles. "Just remind me that they're not in third-grade, yet."

Use the five whys to work with your child to discover the root of a problem. Remember to work with children, and resist the urge to fix a situation.

Who Owns the Problem?

Five-year-old Samantha leaves her lunchbox at home at least once a week. Her mother, Lori, makes a special trip to school to bring Samantha's lunch—a thirty-minute disruption to Lori's day.

Who owns the problem of getting Samantha's lunch to school? Samantha or her mother?

Some parents feel that they own all their children's problems. When we take responsibility for every one of our children's actions we are robbing our children of the opportunity to grow more responsible and to understand the consequences of their actions or inactions.

If the child owns the problem, we should let the child handle the problem, but support the child as necessary.

If the parent owns the problem, then we must work with the child in order for the child to learn from the experience and become more responsible.

We can determine who owns the problem by asking the following questions:

1. Who is directly affected with this situation?

2. Who is the person complaining or making an issue of the situation?

3. Whose work is being undermined?

In the forgotten lunch situation of Samantha and Lori, both Samantha and Lori are directly affected, along with others in Samantha's classroom. Samantha pouts and refuses to join in classroom activities, thus disturbing her classmates, until she can call her mother to bring her lunch.

Samantha is the major complainer in this situation. Lori isn't thrilled, either, about having to take another 30 minutes out of her morning to get lunch to school.

Lori's work is being undermined by Samantha's forgetfulness, while Samantha's work of becoming more responsible is not being developed.

Samantha should own the problem of remembering her lunch and suffer the consequences of having to eat school lunch on the days she forgets her lunch. Lori can work with Samantha to help Samantha learn to independently remember her lunch by using mnemonic devices such placing a note on the backdoor or the backseat of the car.

Our goals as parents should be to help our children develop concentration and independence. Helping our children own their problems prepares our children for the challenges they will encounter in the day-to-day existence of their lives.

Many adults who work with elementary, junior high, high school and college-age students report that parents seem to be running interference for their children far more often than necessary, thus denying their children the chance to learn from solving their own problems. These parents seem to appear immediately out of nowhere to intervene in their children's difficulties, thus earning themselves the nickname of "helicopter parents." Calling teachers about forgotten homework, arguing with coaches about a demerit in sports, hiring consultants to write college applications, to appearing on their children's job interviews on college campuses—every new experience for their children is hovered over by these helicopter parents in misguided search and rescue attempts.

Allow your children to take responsibility for their own problems, while supporting your children as they learn to navigate new waters.

Before jumping in to solve a problem, ask yourself, "Who truly owns this problem?"

If the answer is my child, don't hesitate "to let 'em have it."

Remember: it is only one squiggly letter to go from mothering to smothering.

Stuck With a Problem? SOAR

At times we seem to be ensconced in recalcitrant situations. We try to move forward and our strategy doesn't work. We resolve to get our two-year-old to stop biting. Our ten-year old forgets to clean his room—every Saturday. Our fourteen-year-old refuses to go to church. Whatever we to do to encourage or cajole our children into compliance, well, nothing seems to change except our blood pressure.

As we work through problems with our children, let's remember to include our children in the process. Let's "work with" our children instead of trying to "do to" our children with quick fix manipulations or techniques.

As we consider a situation that needs a remedy, let's try to SOAR. SOAR stands for—Situation. Obstacle. Action. Results.

Look at the Situation. Six-year-old Emily can't seem to find her shoes in the morning, thus making rest of the Decker family late and grumpy getting out the door, creating tension and tears.

Obstacles to Solution. Here are some obstacles Emily's family had in this situation: too many places in the house for shoes to hide; Emily's inflexibility about wearing other shoes; Emily's ten-year-old brother, Tim's, delight in hiding the shoes; Emily's being oblivious of where she removes her shoes.

Actions Taken. Various actions used in trying to solve the situation follow: Emily's parents encouraged Emily to put her shoes in her room; asked Emily to be more flexible about which shoes she wears; designated a special place in the kitchen for Emily's shoes; and requested Tim not to joke around by hiding Emily's shoes.

Results. Even with the actions mentioned above, Emily can't find her shoes, or other vital objects, three out of five mornings. Yelling ensues; Tim and Emily are late for school and/or forget their lunches due to the stress.

What became evident to Bob and Marge in the SOAR process was that the problem was not Emily and her shoes. The overriding problem Bob and Marge discovered was that the peace and love within their family was being eroded.

Bob and Marge's next step was to call a family meeting to problem solve with Tim and Emily using a five-step format.

Step 1. Recognizing that you have a problem.

Step 2. Identifying the problem.

Marge and Bob recognized and identified a problem using SOAR. Bob and Marge started the family meeting with a simple statement: "We think we have a problem that needs some solving. This is how we see the problem. We want our mornings to be peaceful and loving so that we all leave for school and work without feeling edgy and upset. Do you see this as a problem too? How can we make our mornings more peaceful?"

Step 3. Brainstorming for solutions. The Deckers came up with ideas such as getting up 10 minutes earlier, putting out clothes the night before, going to bed earlier, banning practical jokes in the morning and being committed to calm mornings.

Step 4. Choosing the best solution. The Deckers decided that most of their headaches were due to clothing issues so they decided to work on getting clothes ready the night before.

Step 5. Is it working? Each day the Deckers recorded on their calendar a "P" for Peaceful or a "T" for Tense. After a week the Deckers could see that their plan was working and made refinements as needed.

The Deckers didn't let a bad situation get them down. They SOARed by looking at the situation, obstacles, actions and results they had already obtained to help them discover a larger problem. Bob and Marge included their children in problem solving, brainstorming to find solutions, choosing the best solution as a family and then implementing and monitoring their solution.

No Quick Fix

We all look for it. It's human nature to search for the easy way out, the fast buck, and the simplest or cheapest solution.

In human relationships there is no quick fix. Mutual trust and respect must form the foundation of any successful relationship. Without trust and respect, relationships flounder, and eventually whatever natural bonds exist unravel.

As parents and adults, in our relationships with children, we must bring with us the utmost trust and respect for the child and our relationship. We must trust and respect the work of the child in his or her efforts to build a unique human being. The child's life is totally dependent on his or her adult relationships. The adults in a child's life create the conditions for the child's self-construction. A breakdown in the critical underpinnings of those adult/child interactions adversely affects the child.

When we experience a child doing what he or she "ought not" or being "naughty," we need to realize that the child has lost an essential connection to an important adult in his or her life. A misbehaving child is trying to communicate that he or she has lost vital trust and respect with an adult.

Seeking answers on how to deal with our children, we take parenting classes, read books and advice columns, and visit with other parents. The easy solution is not to be found there.

We learn communication techniques, such as active listening, I-messages, logical consequences, etc. to try to solve our problems with children. These tools can help if used in a spirit of trying to work with our children instead of trying to put a bandage on a floundering relationship. Effective communication skills depend on an underlying foundation of mutual trust and respect.

Many times our difficulties with children stem from a deficiency of personal trustworthiness and respectfulness in our relationship. Trustworthiness is created by a combination of character and competence.

Character is comprised of three basic qualities: integrity, maturity and generosity. When we can make and keep promises to ourselves and to others, we have integrity. Maturity comes when we have experienced the effort and effect of keeping our promises and can deal with problems with kindness and compassion. Generosity comes from a belief that there are plenty of resources to go around and that mistakes are only setbacks in reaching our objectives.

A person of character can walk their talk with kindness and compassion while possessing a generous spirit.

Competence, the other component of trustworthiness, requires practical skills, the ability to see the big picture and an understanding that all things are interrelated. With competency, we know how to do something; we know why we are doing it; and we understand how it connects to the bigger picture, either now, or in the future.

Respect, a cornerstone for successful relationships, literally means to look again from its Latin roots of *re+spectare*. With respect, we look a person in the eye and the person looks back. The relationship connects through the eyes. With just a look we show respectfulness while non-verbally communicating, "I think you are a worthwhile human being." To get respect, we have to give respect.

A misbehaving child is a discouraged child, a child looking and not finding trustworthiness and respectfulness in an essential adult relationship. When navigating rough waters and unknown territory in your adult/child relationships think about why a child may have lost a vital connection to your trust and respect, then work to re-establish that trust and respect.

Relationships are built with character, competence and respect. There is no easy way.

APPENDIX

A Note about Dr. Maria Montessori and Montessori Education

In this book I make several references to Dr. Maria Montessori. I have been a Montessori teacher for over twenty years and have been involved in Montessori work through my children for almost thirty years.

You may ask, what is Montessori education?

Here is an excerpt from my book, *Understanding Montessori: A Guide for Parents:*

In its simplest form, Montessori refers to the philosophy of child and human development as presented by Dr. Maria Montessori, an Italian physician who lived from 1870 to 1952.

In the early 1900s, Dr. Montessori built her work with mentally challenged children on the research and studies of Jean Itard and Edward Seguin. Itard is known for his work with Victor, the "Wild Boy of Aveyron," an eleven-year-old found in the woods of France in 1799. Victor lacked spoken language skills and is presumed to have survived without human interaction. Itard's work established the idea that language can only be learned early in life. Itard also designed hands-on language materials for teaching Victor, materials that Dr. Montessori further developed.

Seguin expanded Itard's work with deaf children and designed hands-on materials for understanding basic mathematics. In 1907, at the behest of the Roman Association for Good Buildings, Dr. Montessori began using her teaching materials, based on Itard's and Seguin's designs, with normal children in a Rome tenement. Working with those children Dr. Montessori discovered what she called the "Secret of Childhood."

What is the secret? Children love to be involved in self-directed, purposeful activities. When given a specially prepared learning environment of meaningful hands-on projects, along with the time to do those projects at his or her own pace, a child will choose to engage in activities that will create learning in personal and powerful ways.

A Montessori prepared environment includes the outdoors as well as the indoors and is filled with time-tested, hands-on materials that meet specific learning needs and encourage positive brain development. Above all, Montessori prepared environments are attractive to children and peaceful, giving children a place to learn and grow in grace and dignity.

Dr. Montessori's principles of child and human development are so much a part of my life and my family's life that I find it impossible not to refer to these principles in my writings.

Montessori principles form the plan for my cathedral.

Bibliography

Carnegie, Dale. *How to Win Friends and Influence People* (Pocket) 1998.

Clark, Evelyn. *Around the Corporate Campfire* (Insight Publishing) 2004.

Covey, Stephen R. *The Seven Habits of Highly Effective People* (Simon and Schuster) 1989.

Covey, Stephen R. *The Seven Habits of Highly Effective Families* (St. Martin's Griffin) 1998.

Covey, Stephen R. *The Eighth Habit* (Free Press) 2004.

DeBono, Edward. *Six Thinking Hats* (MICA Management Resources) 1985.

DePree, Max. *Leadership is an Art* (Broadway Business) 2004.

Dyer, Wayne W. *What Do You Really Want for Your Children?* (Quill) 1985.

Faber, Adele and Mazlish, Elaine. *How to Talk So Kids Will Listen and Listen So Kids Will Talk* (Avon Books) 1980.

Gordon, Thomas. *Parent Effectiveness Training* (Peter H. Wyden) 1973.

Gottman, John. *Raising an Emotionally Intelligent Child* (A Fireside Book) 1998.

Gottman, John. *The Relationship Cure* (Three Rivers Press) 2001.

Hannaford, Carla. *Smart Moves: Why Learning Is Not All in Your Head* (Great Ocean Publishers) 1995.

Healy, Jane M. *Your Child's Growing Mind* (Broadway) 1987, 1994.

Jensen, Eric. *Enriching the Brain: How To Maximize Every Learner's Potential.* (Jossey-Bass) 2006.

King, Ross. *Brunelleschi's Dome.* (Penguin) 2001.

Kohn, Alfie. *Punished by Rewards: The Trouble with Gold Stars, Incentive Plans, A's, and Praise and other Bribes* (Houghton Mifflin) 1993.

Levine, Mel. *A Mind at a Time* (Simon and Schuster) 2002.

Louv, Richard. *Last Child in the Woods: Saving Our Children From Nature Deficit Disorder* (Algonquin Books) 2005.

Macaulay, David. *Cathedral* (Houghton Mifflin) 1973.

Montessori, Maria. *The Absorbent Mind* (ABC-Clio Ltd.) Oxford, England: 1949, 1988.

Montessori, Maria. *The Discovery of the Child* (Ballantine Books) New York: 1967.

Montessori, Maria. *The Secret of Childhood* (Ballantine Books) New York: 1966.

Leopold, Aldo. *A Sand County Almanac* (Ballantine) 1990.

McGraw, Phillip. *Family First* (Free Press) 2004.

Paley, Vivian Gussin. *You Can't Say You Can't Play* (First Harvard University Press) 1993.

Popkin, Michael. *Active Parenting* (Active Parenting Press) 1983.

Seligman, Martin E. P. *The Optimistic Child* (Houghton Mifflin) 1995.

Seligman, Martin E. P. *Authentic Happiness* (Free Press) 2002.

Shaw, Robert. *The Epidemic: The Rot of American Culture, Absentee and Permissive Parenting, and the Resultant Plague of Joyless, Selfish Children* (Reganbooks) 2003.

Acknowledgements

Thank you to the following for use of graphics:

Cover Image:
Builders at Work (taken from a 15th century manuscript) from Aubrey, William Hickman Smith: "The National and Domestic History of England" (1878)
www.fromoldbooks.org

Illuminated letters:
http://retrokat.com/medieval/lech.htm
Children's Alphabet by Hans Weiditz, Augsburg 1521

Labyrinth Image:
John E Ridder, www.paxworks.com, www.labyrinthshop.com, www.labyrinths.org, www.peacefulsites.com

About the Author

Maren Stark Schmidt

Maren Schmidt currently writes the award-winning newspaper column on child development issues, Kids Talk. She is a certified Association Montessori Internationale (AMI) elementary practitioner. Ms. Schmidt founded a Montessori school in 1991 and has over twenty-five years experience working with children. She is the author of *Understanding Montessori: A Guide for Parents.*

During those years Schmidt taught children, from ages two to fifteen years, acting as school administrator, curriculum coordinator, and parent education coordinator, as well as being a classroom teacher. She has also worked for several years as a parenting instructor using the Active Parenting curriculum.

Schmidt holds a M.Ed. in Curriculum and Instruction from Loyola College in Baltimore, Maryland. She attended the University of Arkansas at Little Rock, earning a degree in Interpersonal and Organizational Communications.

Schmidt resides in Welches, Oregon with her husband, Mark. She is the mother of two daughters, Dana and Hannah.

At present, Schmidt divides her professional time between writing, speaking and consulting on Montessori and child development topics.

Visit www.MarenSchmidt.com for more information.

.